EVERYONE'S CRAZY
EXCEPT YOU AND ME...
AND I'M NOT
SO SURE ABOUT YOU

EVERYONE'S CRAZY
EXCEPT YOU AND ME ...
AND I'M NOT
SO SURE ABOUT YOU

LIONEL

HYPERION NEW YORK

Library of Congress Cataloging-in-Publication Data

Lionel
Everyone's crazy except you and me—
and I'm not so sure about you / by Lionel.
p.   cm.
ISBN 978-1-4013-0366-2
1. American wit and humor. I. Title.
PN6165.L56 2008
818'.5402—dc22
2008020568

Hyperion books are available for special promotions, premiums, or corporate training. For details contact Michael Rentas, Proprietary Markets, Hyperion, 77 West 66th Street, 12th floor, New York, New York 10023, or call 212-456-0133.

FIRST EDITION

10 9 8 7 6 5 4 3 2 1

May 2009

To my Inamorata

CONTENTS

Contents

Contents

ACKNOWLEDGMENTS

I thank my parents, who always encouraged and believed in me and marinated me in love. To my sisters, I'm sorry for suggesting you were adopted and that the police brought you; you weren't adopted. I thank my managers, Jeff Schwartz and Ian Heller, whose incredible success today would be impossible were it not for my having given them their start. To my editrix, Brenda Copeland, thank you for your brilliant guidance and Canadian sensibility. And to my son, I am so proud of you and love you madly.

EVERYONE'S CRAZY
EXCEPT YOU AND ME...
AND I'M NOT
SO SURE ABOUT YOU

I HATE CONSERVATIVES

I hate conservatives. Hate 'em. Yes, I know, *hate* is a strong word. That's why I use it. But bear in mind: I'm speaking of the *faux* conservative, the dude who has co-opted and hijacked the word. The Rush Limbaugh wannabe. The demented radio and TV ideologue who *thinks* he knows what the term means. It's ideological larceny plain and simple. Would you prefer loathe, detest, abhor? Okeydoke. I loathe, detest, and abhor these faux conservatives. In fact, they make me sick. They are the bane of my very existence. They are a waste of flesh and the fact that we share DNA astounds me to no end. They fit somewhere on the phylogenetic tree between autochthonous tree sloth and soap dish. And it's not a tight fit.

Knuckle-draggers.

Mouth-breathers.

Faux conservatives are uneducated and uninformed. Their main source of sustenance is hate. Hate fueled by fear and ignorance. Hate inspired by a vision of the America that will come about if the nonconservatives have their way. Environmentalists and gays and trannies. Oh my! Freethinking liberals and progressives whose beliefs are based on science, nature, and fact. The horror! Fear fueled by the horror that's been promised them by the faux conservative leaders if they don't pay attention to the alarm that demands obeisance to all that is, well, conservative. They are bumper-sticker, sound-bite, echo-chamber, cookie-cutter, stenographic RNC acolytes, sycophants, bootlickers, and toadies. They're conservative-lite.

Have I made myself clear?

The faux conservative believes in all that is contained in his playbook, the superficial list of formations, the shorthand of what to say when asked. First and foremost, he must understand that title means everything. To qualify as a conservative—to be a member of the club—he must commit to memory all of the beliefs of the faux conservative. He must be able to recite those beliefs. But who cares what beliefs actually mean? These lamebrains couldn't tell you what they're conserving. Remember, it's the label that's important, not the core understanding and knowledge that should come with wearing the conservative badge. These nitwits are Republicans at best, and even that ideology they're not so sure about. They just want to give you that shit-eating grin and snotty sneer when they announce proudly that they're conservative. Translation: I'm a true-blue, red-blooded, rock-ribbed, all-American. I'm the backbone of this country. But these invertebrates have no backbone. They are spineless twits—all talk with no articulable beliefs. All hat. No cattle.

The conservative label provides the faux conservative with arrogance. It inspires an immeasurable pride. If only it inspired an understanding of what the conservative label really meant. Alas . . .

The problem is, Americans love labels. Anything that enables immediate identification is just dandy with us. As much as we like to believe that it's a good thing to "think outside the box" (and Jesus, do I hate that phrase), we look for the box every chance we get—and then we stick a great big old label on it. Give us a shortcut or shorthand, anything that speeds up the conversation and dulls the analysis, and we're happy. It's the autocomplete analogue. If autocomplete is enabled in your computer's Web browser, go online, type a few key letters or phrases in the address bar or search engine, and watch as the browser fills in the blanks, mistakenly "thinking" that it knows whereof you speak. Warning: This can be most unsettling to the less-than-understanding wife who finds "shaved Asian babes" when she was searching for "shared responsibility." Google that.

Back to the conservatives.

Let me be clear. I'm not talking about the conservative who has been around since Methuselah or the conservatism espoused by William F. Buckley, Jr., Barry Goldwater, and Saint Ronald Reagan. That conservatism was actually comprised of a system of beliefs, with tenets, planks, and platforms. Those conservatives actually believed in the concept of limited government. Heck, touting it was their primary focus. Taxes, regulation, bureaucracy . . . you name it, they wanted to limit it, with the exception of defense. No conservative ever wanted to limit that. But who in the hell is *against* defense?

I am a firm believer in many classically conservative concepts and tenets. They border on libertarianism, a term almost universally misunderstood because of the *liber* prefix. To the latter-day radio and TV conservative this sounds too much like *liberal*, much as *vet* sounds to a dog like "Let's lop off his balls."

The term *conservative* has been hijacked by virtually everyone in today's talk radio. As if that weren't bad enough, without exception, those purveyors of conservatism couldn't explain the concept if you held a gun to their mother's head. Or their mother's gun to their head. Sorry to say, but these days the term is a mere diagram for a very simple collective image: true-blue, all-American, patriotic, God-fearing, heterosexual, conventional, family-centered, old-fashioned, tried-and-true, down-to-earth, flag-waving, John Wayneesque, Christian, Reagan-adoring, good, historically representative, WHITE Republican.

Today's conservative loves country music—make that bad country music. Corn pone and cornball. Hokum and bunkum. The Johnny Mann Singers can do no wrong. Mayberry, baby.

Today's conservative? Think anything Franklin Mint. Cheesy. A Dale Earnhardt commemorative clock would be a great stocking stuffer for the faux con. He probably has in his collection every Lee Greenwood CD. You know, Lee Greenwood, the "God Bless the U.S.A." guy. See, the faux conservative loves unambiguous song titles and messages. But this can prove to be problematic. Remember when Saint Reagan loved Bruce Springsteen's "Born in the U.S.A."? What conservative in his right mind wouldn't just love a catchy title like that? But in keeping with the superficiality of the con, it seems that the Gipper never actually listened to the lyrics nor did anyone on his staff. The song speaks of a depressing and dreary America that shortchanges its citizens and veterans. But it does have a catchy title.

Today's conservative yearns for the good old days, a halcyon period that never existed in the first place. The American flag is his fetish. The semiotics of his beliefs include a

Frank Capra vision of the most basic and trite hyperpatriotism.

I could devote an entire chapter to flag fetishism and the people who wrap themselves in it, often literally. Look at the covers of any of these cretins' books; the flag is always prominently featured. It's the red, white, and blue through and through. But it's not your flag, it's theirs. Make no mistake about it, buckaroo. It's their country. You're just visiting.

These cretins believe that any Republican-originated war is warranted, beneficial, and efficacious in preserving "our freedom." Yep. Wanton violence and the senseless slaughter of American military in Iraq are somehow connected to preserving freedom here. See, there's this conflation of all wars, noble and unnecessary. World War II was certainly critical in quashing Hitler. God knows he posed a significant threat to us. What he'd want with Cleveland, I don't know, but, yeah, WWII was certainly freedom-connected. But Iraq? The faux conservatives know as much about logic as they do history.

In fact, one of their favorite post–9/11 mantras was "better to fight them there than here." They have such a unique sense of how our enemies think. See, Ahmed and Moqtada were about to take the shuttle to Des Moines to wreak havoc, rape our women, and eat our children (not to mention our cheese), but since that pesky invasion took place, they're now hunkered down in Tikrit, their plans of destruction gravely interrupted.

Rubbish!

How about this beaut? "There hasn't been a 9/11 since 9/11." Think about this canard. (Why was there a 9/11 in the first place? Don't get me started on that one.) The faux conservative posits that the nonoccurrence (or non-reoccurrence) of an event is due to a quantifiable factor. Bullshit.

It is not always possible to say why something *did not* happen. For example, I've never had scurvy. I've never had a safe fall on my head. That weird mole never sprouted hairs. Why? Because I live in New York. Because I stopped smoking. Because I wear glasses. Because I don't wear underwear. Simple, right? Don't kid yourself. (Sometimes I do wear underwear.) Want another example? OK. Assume that you are burgled. You then purchase a burglar alarm system. No further burglaries occur. To what do you attribute this non-reoccurrence? The new burglar alarm system or my not wearing underwear?

Conservatives have claimed exclusive ownership of all that is American. They grab the best symbols: the flag, the Bible, God, the family, the cross. They would have tried to use the smiley face but that was taken. They'd likewise have a hard time with the ♥ symbol as in "I ♥ the U.S.A.," because conservatives have no ♥. The other side, the dark side, the dreaded liberal viewpoint has grabbed these doozies: abortion, euthanasia, flag *burning*, gays, transgenders, evolution, atheism. (We'll get back to the imaginary liberal later.)

Conservatives see no gray. Black and white, baby. A ham-fisted, apodictic, and Manichean worldview that sees it all quite simply: us versus them; good versus bad; right versus wrong; my way or the highway. (Can you say *Dubya*?) These guys are absolutely correct about everything they think they espouse. Stubborn, hardheaded. No, bullheaded.

The term *alternative* doesn't exist in the lexicon of the faux conservative. That would suggest variation, or worse, deviation. That would allow wiggle room. Worse still, it would signal indecision and a lack of steadfastness. Alternative lifestyle? You're a perv. Alternative energy source? You're a tree-hugger. The notion of maybe, perhaps, or kinda doesn't register with the faux conservative. He sees the world as the rest of us see pregnant and dead.

The conservative I hate the most is the prototypical angry white guy. Always pissed off, always frightened, his world is under attack from gays, immigrants, and transgender freaks, all of whom want to burn our flag, er, his flag, supplant his native tongue, dilute his culture, rape his wife, and eat his children. His way of life is under attack. To this Neanderthal, alternative anything augurs destruction. Sodom and Gomorrah here we come. Giving in to anything, allowing any leeway invokes the dreaded specter of the slippery slope. There's no room for concession in these troglodytes' "minds."

You see, these faux cons believe that gay marriage will lead to the end of traditional marriage. Gay acceptance will lead to ephebophilia as a national pastime. What next?, they query. Passive necrophilia? Urolagnia? Frottage? Philately? Would you want *your* daughter to be a thespian?

Relaxing standards for a second will lead to the unraveling of their America, their tiny, uptight, and closeted myopic world. They fear losing their culture and language despite the forty-third President's persistent references to the imaginary *nucular* threat. (A cacoepy not originated by Dubya, but now made famous by him.)

Mention illegal immigration and the Cro-Magnon conservative envisions the serape-clad, sombrero-totin' Pedro and his fifteen brown kids crossing the Rio Grande and infecting our pristine culture with reasonably priced fruit. And make no mistake about it: The issue of illegal immigration is all about the brown guy, the Mexican. The debate is fueled by not-so-latent racism and xenophobia. Don't believe it? George Bush Sr. may have declared his love for "the little brown ones" (three of his grandchildren), but still, you've got to ask yourself where the hue and cry would be if we were talking about the Swedish Bikini Team crossing our borders and "diluting" our culture.

Fear is the underlying motivation and fuel that energizes these microcephalics. One commentator frequently speaks of the ills of hip-hop music—how it lauds ho's and bitches and waxes romantic about pimps and gangbangers. This fool has nary a clue of what he speaks, but if he can convey the image of the gold-toothed, bling-adorned, doo rag–sportin', hypermentulate Mandingo who lusts for your daughter, all the while infecting the counterfeit conservative's pristine American world with ghetto gibberish, he wins. He wins by spreading his hate-and-fear virus, all under the guise of conservatism and American values.

The archetypal faux conservative is sex-obsessed. Anything short of Nelson Eddy, missionary, blah intromission scares the bejesus out of him. And when it comes to gays— and let's be frank, it's gay men he fears—anal sex is a persistent preoccupation. He can't get it off his mind. Buggery fascinates him. He obsesses over it. Oh, he'll try to attribute this fear to the spread of AIDS and the like (as if that were OK), but don't be fooled. He perseverates in this obsession like a cow smelling water off a long drive. And let's not forget the "doth protest too much" admonition. The faux conservative's preoccupation speaks of an underlying sexual-identity conflict. There can be no other explanation.

And talk about mean.

The talk radio faux conservative takes mean to an art form. Mean, nasty, rude. There's no such thing as discourteous. They're social misfits. Go down the list in your mind. Can you think of one of their ilk who's even remotely warm and fuzzy? Not to mention funny. Funny to them is derision and mockery. The DSM-IV should include them among its recognized psychological maladies.

I hate these people.

Did I already mention that?

But who am I kidding?

I actually love these guys. They have provided me with hours of show topics and analysis. They are a bottomless well of great material. There's nothing they can say that's too over the top.

Now, the target of their wrath is the ultimate straw man. A veritable Potemkin village personified. An ideological bogeyman. The source of our problems, the virus that infects our society, the scourge that is responsible for moral erosion, is the dreaded liberal. This personification of abject evil and immorality is the subject of their railings.

Let me describe this villain whose destruction is the idiot conservative's *raison d'être*. But first a word about the necessity of the evildoer.

Man must have something and someone to hate. Don't let anyone fool you; it's more fun to hate. (Just look at the fun I'm having now.) A society, country, government, name it, must have an enemy: someone or something that threatens its very survival. We've had Pinkos, Russkies, and Commies. Krauts, Japs, and Charlie. We've had Keebler Elves, munchkins (members of the proto-socialist Lollipop Guild), and Lucky Charms leprechauns. While enmity directed at faith or melanin is verboten, it's quite all right to focus loath-ing on something or someone that is perceived to pose a real threat to our way of life. Hatred projected toward a target defines who the haters are.

Add to our hate hit list terrorists and gays for they both seek to undermine what is sacred and essential to us. But if you feel uncomfortable with hating them (or less than sure-footed in your directed contempt), aim your fury at . . . the Dreaded Liberal.

Just who, you might ask, is the dreaded liberal?

Let me give you the comic-strip composite.

The dreaded liberal is an atheist. He hates God and peo-ple who worship. Calling him godless doesn't scratch the surface. In fact, he loves it. He has no moral values, no moral code. A sexual profligate, his life is one long interconnected roll in the hay, one long series of debauched depravity. He's a drug-taking, dope-smoking sot. A satyr of the first order. A slaggard, a dipsomaniac. A tree-hugging environmentalist pansy whose sole fealty is pledged to unrealistic claims that mankind is the basis for the destruction of the planet.

The dreaded liberal is a Birkenstock-shod, tie-dyed effete. He eats organic gruel. He cares more about harp seals than unborn fetuses. He is a card-carrying member of PETA and the ACLU, two incalculably nefarious organizations whose sole purpose is the destruction of all that is American and good. He loathes the killing of animals for their fur and, get this, global warming, the greenhouse effect, and climate change. Imagine! He recycles everything.

Bastard.

When it comes to war, the dreaded liberal hates our troops. His patron saint is Cindy Sheehan, an obvious Commie sympathizer who is a double agent for al Qaeda. He's a pacifist, a weak, impuissant coward. He's a traitor. His incessant refrain anent war and death gives aid and comfort to "the enemy," an amorphous cabal of fill-in-the-blank bad guys and desperadoes. There's nothing better for a liberal than to spend a warm afternoon with arms locked, swaying to the beat of "Give Peace a Chance," all the while flashing that insipid peace sign.

Liberalphobia has become a veritable cottage industry for many of the imaginationally challenged hosts and commentators. Screeds, books, polemics. Nonsensical, repetitious blatherings about this dreaded scourge.

But who are these people? Who are the dreaded liberals? Where do they live? Let's find them and arrest them. I'm all for it. After all, if you can find just one person roaming our planet today who possesses just 10 percent of these characteristics, I'll be the first to demand their immediate incarceration.

Sorry, Virginia: There may be a Santa Claus, but there are no liberals. They're the collective figment of the fearmongers' minds. These liberal monsters sell books (let's hope they sell mine) and provide instant targets for the counterfeit conservative. These people don't exist in any appreciable size or number in the real world. Fear not. They're *de minimis*.

The dreaded liberal was created as the bogeyman. A straw man who has come to stand for everything the faux conservative is against, the liberal is a political tourist attraction, like Bigfoot or the Loch Ness Monster. The dreaded liberal lets the conservative off the hook by symbolizing all that he is against. Know what you're against and you're relieved of the effort to come up with something that you're for. And by the way . . . I don't know anyone who actually calls himself a liberal. Nobody calls himself a pervert, either. It's that label thing again.

Want more good news?

The counterfeit conservative doesn't exist in the real world either. Most Americans are rational. Realistic. Kind. Feeling. Sentient. We share a broad spectrum of views and ideas.

Good news? No. Great news.

Don't believe me? Try this—it's a thought experiment that the counterfeit, bumper-sticker conservatives can't handle.

Think of a football field and you're at the fifty-yard line. Dead even. Right down the middle. Neither conservative nor liberal. Neither red nor blue. Neither nothing.

You're pro-choice? That's liberal. Move one yard to the left.

You're against the death penalty? Liberal. Move another yard to the left.

You hate big and intrusive government. Move one yard to the right. Wait! Is that conservative or liberal or even libertarian? You hate big government when it comes to taxes, but love it when it limits *their* sexual freedom.

But, wait. You're against the death penalty but you support the Pope. He also is pro-life/anti-choice. Surely the Pope's not a liberal, or is he? Wait! Where do I move? When do I lose my liberalness? Or did I?

Stop! Everyone stop. There's nothing more stultifying than this trite and silly labeling. So just stop.

Did I mention that I hate conservatives?

PROFESSIONAL WRESTLING
CHANGED MY LIFE

Good guy. Bad guy. Heel vs. Baby-Face. Good vs. Evil. It
sounds simple, but it was anything but. I loved the blood,
the passion and, yes, the athleticism. I was a kid when I first
turned on to professional wrestling. It scared me witless and
I loved it. The torrents of blood and sweat. (Rarely tears,
though.) Hulking brutes your dad's age thrashing around in
trunks and knee pads, all the while beating the living crap
out of each other. And for what? For nothing. For no reason.
Most times not even for a belt or a title. Minimal prestige.

They were there to beat the living shit out of each other.

They were there for my entertainment.

Got to love that.

Professional wrestling taught me all about the art of illusion. It taught me that even though I should never give in to

the obvious, I could give in to my imagination. Don't believe that these two people are killing each other, just imagine they are. It's okay to suspend disbelief . . . as long as you know you are doing it. When you watch a movie, you know it's not real. Sure, it's violent and filled with gratuitous gore, but it's on a screen and there was a director who yelled "Cut!" and credits rolled. You even saw the stars of the film give interviews.

Pro wrestling was like a movie, but so much better. It was live, for starters. There was an unconscious man in front of you and he was bleeding real blood. No special effects here. No stuntmen. Before the unconscious man was unconscious he was so close to you that you were often showered with his sweat, not to mention the array of phlegmy goo he'd spit when hit. (Am I making you hungry?) This was no movie. No one was about to yell "Cut!" The only cuts were on this poor bastard's head. But it wasn't really real. It was choreographed real. Orchestrated mayhem. And it was OK to watch. These weren't Christians and this wasn't ancient Rome. You knew somehow that this insanity was scripted, or at least that no one would be killed or arrested. But still, you couldn't believe your eyes.

Give the people what they want.

They'll believe anything if you do your job.

That's showbiz, folks!

There has never been a morality play the likes of sixties

and seventies professional wrestling. What's seen today is second tier. Today's wrestlers are too trained, too muscular, and too predictable. Today's wrestler with his incredible, steroid-fueled physique loves the acrobatic move. The wrestler of today thinks he's satisfying my bloodlust by flying through the air and dropping unbelievable heights without crippling injuries. But he's not close to what was then. No, it was the beer-bellied hulk of the sixties—who couldn't somersault to save his life—who just wowed me by scraping barbed wire across his already-scarred forehead and providing torrents of stuck-pig "juice" for my adolescent pleasure. If you were lucky and could score a ringside seat, you'd take home a nice sampling of hemoglobin, completely unaware of bloodborne thingamajigs like hepatitis and staph.

There was nothing flashy about his moves. Some were so base and brutal, they had no names. One wrestler used to just stretch his opponent's mouth open as far as possible. Another would stick anything, repeat, anything into the throat of his opponent—thumbs, pencils, railroad spikes. And as a kid I'd scream at the referee, begging him to do something. Anything! I'll never forget seeing one wrestler's false teeth fall out and watching his opponent smash them to smithereens. Imagine watching this. And you're ten.

Old-style sixties wrestling was more absurd and, frankly, hysterical. And yet, as much as it was ridiculous, it somehow seemed plausible. Imagine a 250-pound subliterate man hitting you repeatedly on the jaw for an hour. Imagine how you'd feel. Imagine the trauma and certain brain damage. It would take you months to recuperate in a hospital with a round-the-clock vigil by your family. Then there would be physical therapy and myriad depositions, the result of litigation that would most probably follow. You wouldn't be able to recognize your family, make a fist, or control your bowels for a good year.

Yet these two gladiators would meet the next night, twenty miles down the road, and do it all again. Defying reality. God, I loved it.

That's just not the way it is today. Vince McMahon and his WWE killed wrestling. Thanks for nothing, Vince. You cleaned it up, schmaltzed it up, and packaged it like McDonald's.

Wrestling then was territorial, thematic, and brilliant.

Wrestling then was "juice" (blood) and "shoots" (the real thing).

Wrestling then was profoundly absurd and absurdly profound. It made sense.

Wrestlers then were out of shape. Dewlapped tenterbellies would strut around and gasp for air at the slightest movement. They may have been aerobically unfit, but they were "workers," an honored title bestowed on but a few of the best.

As for wrestling now? Don't even bother. *The View* is more entertaining.

Wrestling now is too devoted to the pretty boy or the hideously grotesque. Think radio program director, but worse.

Wrestling now is too beholden to sophomoric sex. Somehow these new guys think that a ticket holder will be satisfied with some buxom strumpet "manager."

Wrestling now is not much fun. It's too politically correct, though I hate that term. In my day we had midget, that's right, MIDGET wrestlers. Not little people grapplers but midgets. We also had women, and I use that term loosely, wrestlers. Women who looked like liquor-hardened barmaids. Madams with faces like Buicks and bodies like farm equipment.

I grew up in the Florida of the sixties and seventies when it was a hotbed of superb pro wrestling. Make that *rasslin'*. Florida was NWA territory—that's the National Wrestling Alliance, if you didn't already know. It boasted the best of the best. My hometown of Tampa had no professional sports teams, so pro wrestling was it, and I mean IT! And at the helm of weekly televised wrestling was the absolutely best announcer who has ever lived, the late, great Gordon Solie. He was big. He was box office. He was known everywhere. Gordon was one of my best friends and his death in 2000 still saddens me today. A brilliant man who knew just how to play the audience, especially a little fat kid in Tampa (me), Gordon was absolutely unfazed in his delivery. He was so incredibly deadpan, so serious, that he established the possibility that this ostensible bullshit could be, in fact, real. He was called "the Walter Cronkite of wrestling." I often reminded him that such was not the case; Walter Cronkite was the Gordon Solie of news.

Solie was the hope that there was some legitimacy in this obvious horseshit. He actually seemed distraught when rules were broken. I swear to God, he made me think that there just might be something to all this. Maybe this wild Samoan really is killing Baby-Face. Maybe homicide charges will be waived when he *kills* a man before my eleven-year-old eyes. Gordon took the sanctity and secrets of this sports carnival to heart. No one guarded the mystery that shrouds wrestling better than he did. Today, there is no mystery; there are no secrets. It's all in the open and blatantly so.

Thanks again, Vince McMahon.

Gordon was a master of a unique phraseology. Solieisms (not *solecisms*) made wrestling a blast to watch. I can still hear that delivery.

+ **A Pier 6 brawl.** I have no idea where any pier is, much less Pier 6. And who's brawling?
+ **Neither asking nor giving any quarter.** Got it.
+ **Crimson mask.** A combatant whose face was covered with blood—his own, preferably. And make no mistake about it, the blood was real. Now the fact that it was probably caused by a wrestler autolancing his forehead with a blade of sorts is irrelevant. It was real

blood. To those who suggest that it was chicken blood I have one word for you: *salmonella.*

+ **Katie bar the door.** Don't know just who this Katie is, but I think I have the barred-door concept down.

+ **He's not quick, he's sudden.** Natch.

+ **He was knocked into the next area code (or zip code).** Ditto, natch. This is a variation of knocking someone into next week. *See also* "I'm gonna hit you so hard that when you wake up, your clothes will be out of style."

+ **Quadriceps femoris.** This was Gordon's favorite muscle group. Everything seemed to happen there. The name still frightens me.

+ **The ubiquitous carotid artery.** When the "sleeper" hold was applied, aka "carotid restraint," this baby was cinched, squeezed, clamped, and shunted. Unconsciousness followed thereafter and we were, as always, warned against doing this at home. Where in fact we tried it immediately on an unsuspecting sibling.

+ **Don't try this at home.** This was our signal to indeed try it at home. (See *supra.*) I don't know if Gordon was the first to issue this no-shit warning. I can only imagine the series of incidents that prompted this admonition.

+ **The "foreign object."** As stated, this was something the Heel brought into the ring to be used against his hapless opponent. Foreign objects had nothing to do with any implement that could cause harm. The favorite item retrieved by the scrupulous referee was a tongue depressor covered with athletic tape. I know, I know; I don't get it either.

+ **Catch-as-catch-can.** This seems to be a term for a style of wrestling describing, well, whatever.

+ **From parts unknown, weight unknown.** I loved this phrase. When a masked wrestler entered the ring his identity was concealed. The wrestling announcer would always state that he was from "parts unknown"—OK, I dig that. An obscure town they hailed from might give their identity away. Why they wanted to remain unidentified is still beyond me, but I digress. But their weight? How in the hell would "254 pounds" lead one to an "AHA!" moment? "254! That's Narvell Suggins from Vidalia!" You gotta love this stuff.

+ **The tough but fair-minded ___ (a referee).** I love the idea of a referee who's tough but retains a degree of fair-mindedness. What?! Since when is "fairness" laudable when spoken of a referee? Isn't that the point?

+ **A gentleman both inside and out of the ring.** *Res ipsa.*

+ **Make no mistake about it.** A ubiquitous prefatory statement to virtually anything.

+ **Incredible tendon strength.** This plaudit was accorded to the wrestler Danny Hodge, who, according to Solie, possessed not muscular strength but *tendon* strength. I'm no anatomist or kinesiology expert, but since when does a tendon connote or convey strength? It didn't matter. Danny Hodge would squeeze an apple to smithereens and his tendons were given credit. (Ligament strength? Oh, well.)

+ **The squared circle.** *See* "The ring." Which was in fact a square.

+ **"We'll return when order is restored in the ring."** This was the cue for a commercial. Order was never restored save the order to veer to a commercial.

You may have never heard of Gordon Solie, but you'd be surprised at the millions who have. He was an icon, a god, and a great man that I want to remind the world of. God, I miss him.

Professional wrestling of the sixties and seventies ignored history altogether. My favorite example: The Von Brauners were managed by Gentleman Sol Weingroff. At first blush this may seem like no big deal, but it seems that the Von Brauners were Germans, ostensibly Nazis, who happened to be managed by a Jew. Call me wacky, but I find that hysterical, like Minnie Pearl being managed by Mr. Blackwell.

Wrestling was a morality play. An obvious one at that. The Heel was always obviously evil. He was driven and self-centered, with no concern for rules or the personal safety of his opponent. Baby-Face was the Lone Ranger: truth and justice and the American Way. Unlike serial westerns, Baby-Face could be destroyed on any given day by the Heel. Virtue defeated by the personification of evil. It was a representation of life, a nod to the fact that good guys don't always win. People cheated. Referees missed their calls. A ref could be absolutely a stickler for the most irrelevant and arcane rule, fixated on a wrestler's flouting a nicety, e.g., not having his hand on a turnbuckle while attempting to tag with his partner who was being beaten within an inch of his life, whose brains were being sprinkled about the ring. Not everybody who speeds gets ticketed. Life isn't fair, as the tag team matches made clear.

Oh the horror, the horror. Invariably, Baby-Face is pummeled mercilessly, his face a crimson mask (see page 21). For what seems an interminable time, this hapless gladiator is beaten senseless and approaching brain death in at least twelve states. Then, finally! He makes the tag with his partner and secures that much-needed respite and recuperation while his fresh and very angry tag teammate dispatches the vicious thug. And then, it happens. The ref misses the tag and the beaten, bloody, perhaps brain-damaged wrestler, clinging to life, must return to the ring to endure more punishment unless and until the myopic referee sees the tag. As a kid, watching this drove me crazy. I was such a mark (wrestling term for dumbshit who believed this). I didn't care, I knew that no one would really be hurt and maybe that's a saving grace. Perhaps that removed any pang of guilt over watching what some would consider modern-day human cockfighting. But that makes no sense because (1) a human cannot cockfight unless this book turns pornographic real quick, and (2) cockfighting is real.

But then, when the tag was finally made and the ref finally saw it and the poor bloodied wrestler finally got to rest and recover while his partner avenged his needless carnage, it was orgasmic. I mean, a perfect analogue to sexual climax. Foreplay, foreplay, foreplay, and finally the payoff. The money shot. The happy ending. Justice!

And they say guys don't like foreplay.

One last word about a routine that I must have seen a thousand times. It was classic and Gordon's deadpan was nonpareil. Here goes.

Baby-Face is about to enter the ring to administer justice to some Heel. But before he enters the ring, he wants Gordon to take special care of, say, a lamp that an orphan kid gave him when he made a special visit to some state-run home for, well, orphans, I guess. He implores Gordon to keep an eye on this prized gift from little Jimmy the orphan who's watching while chained to his bed at the home. Gordon assures him that the lamp will be safe.

You know what's coming.

As Baby-Face is tied up dispatching his opponent in the ring, another Heel, usually his main antagonist and rival, comes out and snatches the lamp from a horrified Gordon, who has done virtually nothing to protect the orphan's gift. The Heel taunts Baby-Face—who is inextricably involved with his match—by holding up the prized possession and smashing it to bits, horrifying Baby-Face, the audience, the orphan, and, of course, the man himself. Gordon could convey absolute disgust with a shake of his head. Of course, he and the audience would completely overlook the fact that Gordon didn't lift a finger to stop the inevitable destruction of this precious token of affection from the child who's bound to be heartbroken and crushed over the event. (As I always imagined it, the kid, who is hooked up to some device, is so traumatized by what he sees that he flatlines. OK, I'm sick.) Gordon looks to the camera and mutters a sickened "We'll be right back after order's been restored."

Thank you, Gordon Solie.

THIS IS REALLY BAD

This is one of the most embarrassing moments I've ever experienced. Kinda. Funny, but embarrassing. All right, who am I kidding? It was funny as hell.

After having been in the radio biz for going on twenty years, after having appeared on countless news interview shows and even having my own short-lived show, *Snap Judgment* on Court TV, it's not uncommon for people to recognize me. Yes, I know I have a face for radio, but still, people recognize me and—I swear to God—ask to have a photo taken with me, sometimes an autograph too. It's a part of the biz and if someone is kind enough to ask, I'm not going to be a dick and refuse, even though I always wonder who in hell would want a picture taken with me. So I always courteously oblige the entreaties from the throngs of loyal fans. After all, what is celebrity but having someone recognize you from something you did?

I've had my share of jerk celeb encounters. I'm no Britney or Paris—even though I do share a hobby of videotaping late-night romps through night-vision optics. But it just seems to me that when you go on TV or radio and beg people to watch and listen, the least you can do is not be a royal jerkoff when they dare to acknowledge you. Anyway.

One night I was enjoying a glass of my favorite brown liquid with a great friend of mine in our favorite Irish pub. He is able to back me up on this. If asked, "Where were you on the night of the twelfth?", he would faithfully answer, "Enjoying a glass of brown liquid with Lionel in our favorite Irish pub." OK, so I'm standing at this bar with my back turned to the crowd when a young lady comes over and, some-what embarrassed, asks if she can take a picture. I'll never forget it. She seemed almost in awe, transfixed even. Or maybe transmixed. She looked at me like a dog stares at a hydrant, like George Bush looks at a tax cut. It was a strange look. Dare I say entranced?

Looped, most probably.

Remember, I'm not a dick so I figured *why not?* I turned around to face this very shy young lady and tried to assure her that it was quite OK for her to snap away. I even turned to my friend and said, mockingly cockily, "Ah, the price of fame."

Something was wrong.

She looked confused.

Still, I stood up to allow her to photograph me, the big star. I noticed that there was a woman on one side of me and a very tall man on the other . . . *ah, that's it,* I thought. These two people were trying to horn in on the shot. I assured her it was fine and even suggested that she could crop them out later. I even tried to mutter this under my breath so these two idiots next to me wouldn't be embarrassed. Remember, I'm not a dick.

This poor lass took the shot, all the while looking confused. After all, who were these two people ruining this exclusive shot with me, the big star. After the shot was taken, I even suggested that a second would be a good idea, again reminding her that she could crop out these two photo interlopers. She took a second shot and just walked away. Not a "thank you." Not a "you make my life worthwhile." Not an "I'd like to have your baby." Nothing. And as for the two photo shot intruders?

They were none other than Susan Sarandon and Tim Robbins.

Swear to God.

IT'S THE THOUGHT THAT COUNTS

Americans have this idea that they understand criminal law. They watch *Law & Order*, a show that is to criminal jurisprudence what *M*A*S*H* was to microsurgery. They actually believe that they have a clue as to the fundamentals of law. And the funny-as-shit part is that we are all charged with knowing all laws and what they proscribe. Go figure. We can't claim ignorance; we are supposed to know. And we know *shite*.

First, it is axiomatic that during a criminal prosecution of a victim crime—i.e., a headline-grabbing, blood-and-guts victim crime such as murder, robbery, or rape versus, say, cable theft (which I personally find morally reprehensible)— the prosecutor asks the victim to stand up in court and point out and identify her assailant. (In murder cases, others do this for the stiff.)

It's classic courtroom drama. Identify the scoundrel. It's simple and an absolutely essential element to a crime's prosecution.

"Do you see the man in court who ____ you?"

"Please point to him and identify where he's sitting and what he's wearing."

"Your Honor, let the record reflect that the defendant has been identified."

Cue the "gotcha" theme.

(Personal story inserted: I once saw a woman point out some hapless and very innocent bastard in the courtroom who was only there to be released from incarceration on another charge. He was so enraged by the misidentification that he screamed epithets at the judge and was jailed for an additional six months. On the day he was to be released. Swear to God.)

This isn't just *Law & Order* drama. This is the *sine qua non* of the prosecution. Think about it. Who did it? That creep, Your Honor. Getting the right guy is the foundation of our legal system. How simple. How basic. How logical. How American.

It's the stuff of great television and film drama. Simple, right?

Well, not really.

There's another basic truth that is guaranteed by our Constitution: the Sixth Amendment and its Confrontation

Clause. The duty of the government to prove that the person named in the indictment or charging instrument is indeed the poor schlub sitting there in the courtroom. The right of the accused to confront and cross-examine his accuser and all that. This is basic stuff.

The accused's counsel can then seek to impeach the victim/witness, i.e., to lessen, call into question, or challenge the witness's credibility. In the biz it's called impeachment.

Does he remember the event? Did he really witness it? Is he motivated by some interest that may draw into question his credibility and objectivity? Can he articulate what happened? In legalese, this goes to the competency of the witness. In one famous event, a victim was asked if she was stabbed in the fracas. "No," she replied. "I was stabbed between the belly button and the fracas." Swear to God, it's true.

Basic, right? Well, kinda. It depends.

Enter a new crime: computer cybertrolling for kids via the Internet. We've all heard about it. State legislatures drafted new statutes that made it a crime to communicate naughtily online with people known or believed to be minors. Then *Dateline NBC's* "To Catch a Predator" provided the ultimate in reality TV when it broadcasted local cops enforcing these new laws.

You know the scene.

A forty-five-ish creep goes online and meets someone he

believes to be a fourteen-year-old kid. They engage in sordid IM exchanges over a period of time.

> CREEP: "So, you're 14, huh? Have you ever had the desire to allow a 45-year-old perv to have his way with you? My truck's almost paid for and my mom is out of town this week. The trailer's all mine, lil' lady."
>
> UNDERCOVER COP POSING AS KID: "LOL. ☺ Like, yeah."

The creep sends disgusting images to this person he *believes* to be fourteen. A rendezvous is arranged. The demented cybertroller shows up at a house for a tryst with this person he *believes* to be fourteen, a house that is wired for sound and video and quite possibly popcorn. The e-pedophile shows up and is lured into the trap by the siren call of a decoy who sounds remarkably like Jerry Mathers of *Leave It to Beaver*. Provided, of course, The Beav was into that which is *Beavish*. If you get my drift.

(I must clarify something quickly. This scenario is *not* entrapment. Entrapment takes place when someone is induced to do something he was unwilling to do. Induced by the cops, that is. No one was induced, much less seduced, into this rendezvous by the police. The letch initiated contact on his own. OK, let's proceed.)

As he stands there on camera, the e-pedophile stares nervously at his gifts o' plenty—a six-pack of Budweiser, a couple of cans of Red Bull, a bouquet of gas station flowers, and a pair of Argentinean shackles. All of which explains why this middle-aged man feels he has no other "romantic" options than a person he met on the Internet and *believes* to be fourteen. (I threw in the shackles. Call me crazy.)

Then from behind the door arrives Chris Hansen, the Torquemada of perv probes, who begins to third-degree this pathetic sicko about his intentions and desires. The man is a rabbi, schoolteacher, ex–Navy SEAL, you name it. He cries. He pleads. He begs. He offers a kidney to anyone in the tri-state area; his own, no less. He swears he had no intention of doing anything untoward and that he always carries a gross of luminescent condoms. He further states that the Internet log that Hansen has detailing the explicit online confab is a big mistake. Sure, there were references to his wanting to dress like Harold Stassen and walk in naked save for a dashiki and pince-nez, all the while screaming, "Lafayette, I've arrived!" But he was kidding. Just acting out. This is all a big mistake. You know the drill.

The hapless miscreant then gathers up his portable happy hour, walks out, and is arrested by Joe Friday and a passel of media-hungry cops who scream for numb nuts to freeze and hit the deck. If we're lucky, there's the gratuitous Taser scene (my favorite).

OK, let's jump ahead. It's trial time and Mr. Skeevy is in

the dock. The prosecution puts on its case-in-chief. Detectives testify. Skeevarino looks up and down and perspires conspicuously. Every tawdry and salacious thought ever typed by him in this case is presented to the now sickened jury. IM logs are introduced. Recipes are exchanged.

He's charged with using the Internet to seduce, lure, solicit, cajole, entice, wheedle—use the statutory language of your choice—a child or someone he *believes* to be a child. Repeat: *believes*.

But at trial there's someone missing.

The child.

Where's the fourteen-year-old he *thought* he was chatting with? What? Yeah, the kid. Where is she? He has the right to confront his accuser, right? That pesky Sixth Amendment guarantee of the right to confront your accuser. You know; it was in all the papers, that Bill of Rights thing. There is a kid involved, right?

Not so fast, Cochise. This is a new era. You've entered the world of cybercrime.

The fourteen-year-old was a "what if," a "supposed," a "hypothetical" victim. That's right, Pervball has been charged with *thinking* he was making time with a post-pubescent. He *thought* Trixiegirl69 actually existed.

Sorry, Charlie. It seems the girl of his dreams (literally) is a paunchy forty-five-year-old Palm Beach County detective named Gus. Yeah, Gus, a guy whose idea of a good time is a Coors party ball, lawn darts, and an easy Sudoku. The victim is imaginary. It's like the age-old tenet I learned in Catholic school: If you even think it, you've sinned. It gives *mens rea* a whole new identity and connotation. Just as Jimmy Carter purportedly lusted in his heart, mental sexual reverie is a crime in most states.

Welcome to the thought police and you're guilty.

Now wait.

Lest anyone think I'm in favor of exploiting children, of luring of them through the Internet or carrier pigeon, think again. I am ashamed that I share DNA with pederasts. I have fantasies of exacting medieval torture upon them when they are convicted. I cannot fathom what would compel a human being, a seemingly feeling adult, to exploit a child sexually. There is no prison bad enough for them. May they be forced to watch a continuous video loop of Rachael Ray for the rest of their lives.

That being said, there's a point to be made here. A scary one at that: We're arresting people for their thoughts.

OK, I know what you're thinking. Who cares? We nabbed a perv before he could do something. He probably did this before, and better late than never. What if there had been a kid there? Yeah, yeah. I know.

Listen carefully. This is the sound of a society that fails to think critically and refuses to recognize that a criminal justice system, no matter how well-intentioned, must be watched vigilantly. Just because we nab a creep who thinks of doing the criminal, fantasizes about the sordid, and most probably would have maybe perhaps in the future tried something sick, that doesn't permit us to grab those who illegally think.

Legislators who passed these laws say they had our best interests at heart. Save the kids! It's the stuff of great headlines. It's reelection time; constituents love it. We're still reeling over the Roman Catholic Church's scandals. Pedophilia is a part of our collective top-of-mind awareness. Who could oppose laws against that?

Well, no one.

But what about saving the Constitution? Or saving the basic tenets of due process? Yep, even for a perv.

Here's another beaut.

Take *Ashcroft v. Free Speech Coalition*, please. (Sorry, Henny.) The U.S. Supreme Court struck down a 1996 federal statute that was intended to stop the distribution of materials and images that *appeared* to be kiddie porn. What was *thought* to be child porn. That which looked like and resembled actual child pornography. Think of it as counterfeit child porn.

Now at first blush, that statute sounds great. Who cares if the child porn is real? It matters not that two children depicted in a sordid scene were computer-generated, right? So what if a child's head was Photoshopped onto the torso of an adult—or vice versa. (Now that's sick.) Someone *thought* it was real.

And let's not forget that which is literary. Nabokov's *Lolita*. *Romeo and Juliet*. The Bible. (How 'bout that Lot and his daughters, huh?) In 1900 the Woodsville High School in Haverhill, New Hampshire, removed *Alice's Adventures in Wonderland* from its classrooms because the novel contained references to masturbation and sexual fantasies. In the enlightened 1970s school libraries in Anchorage, Alaska, and Cedar Lake, Indiana, banned due to "objectionable language" a book that any right-thinking person could only consider vile: *The American Heritage Dictionary*.

But do you see? These sorts of actions, and this sort of legislation, represent an attempt by the government to criminalize our perceptions, thoughts, and the like. It's as if the authors of this law really believe that they'll gain five pounds just by looking at that piece of cheesecake.

Kiddie porn should be banned. It is banned. No doubt about it. The Supreme Court has long removed it from any First Amendment analysis. There's no obscenity debate here, folks. Child pornography is just plain verboten. No freedom of expression arguments are relevant. And that's good. Child pornography is the record of an event that was a crime when it occurred, a memorial to a heinous act. Kiddie porn is a frozen moment made available in perpetuity, and as such it subjects the victim to future pain and humiliation. Prohibiting kiddie porn attempts to stifle recurring incidents. This makes perfect sense.

But what about that which *appears* to be kiddie porn, but isn't?

Something that makes you think it's something it's not.

Beware, Constitutionists. Those lawmakers and proponents who "mean well" can slip a prosecution by you that seems so innocuous, so basic, so logical . . . until closer inspection.

Let's think, shall we. Imagine the following: A forty-five-year-old blind man, a tad tipsy, is standing next to a woman he believes is a twelve-year-old underage drinker who's been allowed into a bar. He swears she's twelve. She sounds so young. Maybe she lies and claims to be twelve when she's actually thirty-four. So it's the blonde leading the blind. Our blind man waxes dipsomaniacal and entreats her to get jiggy with him, all the while thinking she's a minor. Assume further they do the nasty. Should he be charged with statutory rape and child endangerment? After all, he *thought* she was twelve.

But where's the victim?

Consider this: A visibly impaired, OK, blind, retired radio program director believes someone is standing next to him on a desolate, poorly lighted street. It's actually a parking meter. He's in need of money and decides to rob the person he believes is there. He pulls out a small-caliber handgun and demands that this person hand over all his cash and valuables. A police officer overhears the rather one-sided exchange and arrests Mr. Magoo for armed robbery. Makes sense, doesn't it? Using today's thought-crime logic, who cares that no one was actually robbed, that there was no actual victim? He thought he was robbing someone. He would have robbed someone had there actually been anybody there. He's probably done it before. He'll probably do it again. Charge him.

OK, now that you're getting the hang of this, let me complicate matters somewhat. The fact is, some erroneous thoughts are subject to criminal sanction and do pass constitutional scrutiny. Say a man arranges a tryst with a young woman he believes to be "legal." He demands four pieces of ID just to be certain. He's presented with a forged driver's license, passport, birth certificate, and Wal-Mart club card. Assume that these pieces of identification are exquisitely and expertly forged, absolutely perfect. This bloke's done everything right, right?

WRONG.

Strict liability laws make statutory rape illegal in most jurisdictions no matter what pains one took to verify age. In this case, ignorance is no defense and belief is irrelevant. Get it? In cybertrolling, if you thought it was a kid you were talking to, good enough. In statutory rape, if you thought, reasonably thought, the lassie was an adult, too bad.

Assume *arguendo* a fifty-four-year-old radio ad exec solicits the murder of his wife in a conversation with a hired and wired hit man who turns out to be an undercover detective.

Talk about a double standard.

Or, a man solicits a prostitute for a moment of scabrous fun. The prostitute is instead an undercover police officer.

Better yet, a woman attempts to buy or sell illicit drugs from or to a drug dealer who is actually a DEA agent.

These examples don't involve mere thoughts. Concrete plans, intentions, and payments are involved and intent is therefore evinced. It matters not that someone believed to be a confederate is actually a cop. The law doesn't require that the confederate be of a certain age or status. The faux co-conspirator's status or position or identity is irrelevant. You merely must (1) intend for an illegal act to be committed (2) with *anyone.* In other words, whenever a statute specifies victim age or status, the victim must be of that group. Crimes against the elderly require an elderly victim. Laws that punish discrimination against the disabled only apply to a disabled victim. Laws that penalize conduct with minors require a victim who's a minor. But in this last case, we've added a new twist: The victim can be someone who's either a minor or someone you *think* is a minor. Think about it. Under this screwy logic, if you abused a twenty-nine-year-old woman you *thought* was seventy-five, you can't be charged with elderly abuse, though you might be referred to an ophthalmologist.

The law says rather clearly that you can't arrange with anyone to have Uncle Wally killed. That's solicitation for murder. No matter who you hire to off him, the crime involved is the *intent* to have him killed. The law also says that you may not solicit anyone for prostitution (Isn't that called dating?). Too bad the floozy you're importuning for paid sex is a detective. The law proscribes the solicitation. It matters not who you thought Miss Kitty was. What matters is that you made an offer, and that offer is what's penalized. Laws don't provide an exception for solicitation; we couldn't care less if she's a commercial trollop.

In drug sales and purchases, it's the sale and purchase attempt that's verboten. Sorry, Charlie, if the buyer or seller you're negotiating with is Kojak, you're SOL. Remember, dear reader, this is not to be confused with conspiracy, an act in which at least two people join together in a plan to commit a crime. Those thoughts aren't imaginary. Those thoughts were a plan to commit a crime, e.g., drug trafficking. There is no imaginary victim here but rather miscreants foiled before a crime could be committed. An actual crime whose "victim" is the state or government.

(For the legal scholars, remember: Conspiracy is never possible with a cop. It must involve at least two "guilty" people. In the dope scenario, you can't be charged with conspiracy to deliver drugs because you can't conspire with a cop.)

One more word on conspiracy, ladies. Lest you believe thoughts are immune from prosecution, making criminal plans is not. Good news, McGruff. If you and I agree that we will commit a crime, even if we never do, we're busted. Notice the delicious semantic variations—wish, desire, thought, belief, plan, intent, agreement. God, I love this stuff.

This is a bit desultory, perhaps, but as a prosecutor I used to laugh when some poor shmuck would sell counterfeit drugs—driveway gravel as crack, aspirin as coke, you name it. The counterfeit controlled substance law made it a more severe crime to sell fugazy junk than the real thing. Think about it. A half ounce of pot: misdemeanor. A half ounce of grass clippings claimed to be pot: felony. Go figure. It's almost a consumer fraud matter. *Caveat emptor*, baby. Please don't ask me why selling bogus shit is punished more harshly than selling the real stuff. I haven't the foggiest.

Here's another example. There is an organization called the North American Man/Boy Love Association (NAMBLA). It is an advocacy group that favors the abrogation of any and all laws that require a minimum age of consent for man-boy sexual endeavors.

Creepy stuff, admittedly. Better yet, creepy thoughts. Weird advocacy. Sick ideas.

When I first heard of NAMBLA, I assumed that it was a fictional organization created by conservative talk show hosts who needed a "no shit" topic. But there seems to in fact be an actual NAMBLA. (I wonder if they have a personalized Visa card with the NAMBLA logo emblazoned thereon.)

Now, suppose a high school teacher, unbeknownst to his

students and faculty colleagues, is a card-carrying member who even pens op-eds and the like favoring the removal of age limitations in sexual activities between adults and children. Assume further that said teacher has no history of improper sexual advances toward his students or any criminal record for that matter. Assume he never speaks of NAMBLA or in any way advocates its positions while at his job.

Then, his advocacy *thoughts* are discovered and he's terminated from his employment as a public school teacher.

Now, think critically. He was fired for his ideas, his thoughts, feelings, opinions. He was terminated for what was in his head, not for anything actually done or committed. He was fired not for breaking the law, but for trying to change it. Our history is replete with abolitionists and their causes. From Prohibition to the legalization of marijuana, people have advocated a new system or the abrogation of an old one via thought. Marijuana laws are still (unfortunately) the law of the land as are sexual age-consent laws. While admittedly they are drastically different in societal impact, the freedom to advocate the change of an extant law is a fundamental right that we as Americans share, but you'd never know it in today's climate.

Should you feel sorry for a NAMBLA member? That's up to you. Should you be alarmed at the broader implications of this scenario? Absolutely. And, by the by, this is not a hypothetical. It's happened. But it generated no alarm, no dissent, no outrage. After all, it was NAMBLA and the thoughts of its members are *per se* perverse and without the ambit of protection of our First Amendment. Or so we claim.

It's very easy to wax pedantic. Funny how a keyboard and a book contract imbues you with Delphic omniscience. But I'm as serious as a heart attack. Left to our own devices, we will legislate away all rights.

And rights are a bitch. You can quote me. This First Amendment stuff seems to always rear its ugly head over nasty subjects and tawdry "expression." That is correct. There has never been an obscenity prosecution brought against the Johnny Mann Singers, though there should have been. There's always some shock jock, porn purveyor, or hip-hop artist who's not content to sing about the beauty of marigolds and how great our country is.

Why can't we all be more like Lee Greenwood and sing sappy paeans to the obvious? Don't know. Why can't Americans just be satisfied with lifeless missionary-style married consensual straight adult sex? Must we troll for porn? The answer is yes, of course. So long as we have synapses and fecund imaginations, so long as the Internet can provide every scabrous permutation of human sexual perversion, we will have some joker making us collectively retch over his lustful expressions.

But, kiddos, liberals and conservatives alike, this systematic erosion of our beloved First, this gradual extension of thought prohibition scares me more than any freak hunched over a keyboard awash in the reverie of smearing brine shrimp on his frenulum whilst a twelve-year-old Taiwanese towel boy whistles "Marching to Pretoria" wearing only a sarong and a smile.

Bumper-sticker, playbook, cookie-cutter, sound-bite, echo-chamber so-called conservatives have never met a law they don't like, especially if it is a law of limitation. Thought, free exercise, personal behavior, you name it. These so-called constitutional strict-constructionists and watchdogs of freedom are anything but. They're in a persistent state of fright and unease. Maybe it's sexual anhedonia. They are perpetually and constantly wary of anyone exercising too much freedom, expression, or experimentation. And if the subject matter of that is anything sexual, as John Gotti would make famous, *fuhgeddaboudit!*

After 9/11 the clarion call was to not let the terrorists win. In New York especially, Rudy Giuliani branded the idea that if we ceased doing *x*, the terrorists win. If we don't shop, carpool, travel, you name it, the terrorists win. Why? Because they hate our freedoms. (I still have nary a clue as to what the hell that means.) But not apparently as much as we do.

Let me make it real simple. If we erode or dilute our precious freedoms in the name of whatever—the wars on crime, terrorism, child exploitation—we'll never get those freedoms back. Freedoms are like limbs; they're not regenerative. There's no sunset provision to amputating freedom of speech. It's under attack—by us. And the ends certainly don't justify the means. I don't care what you say or whom you listen to, *nothing*, no cause or event, is worth destroying what makes us fundamentally American. Nothing. No one. *Nada. Niente. Nihil.*

Should we ever lose our freedoms, it won't be at the hands of invading Visigoths, Islamists, Klingons. No, ma'am. We will have handed them to the government, ostensibly for safekeeping.

Think all you want; watch what you do.

A MAN WALKS INTO A BAR

Everyone should have a bar. Their bar. Within stumbling distance, I might add. Not a fern bar. Not a chichi place, but a joint. A gin mill. A tavern. A barrelhouse. Taproom. Watering hole. Suds shop. A saloon with eau de Pine-Sol. A bartender who calls everyone "Mac."

I have a bar—a pub actually, which is short for "public house," not to be confused with "private house"—that's perfectly ensconced mid-neighborhood. For fourteen years it has been solace, meeting place, union hall, parallel universe. It's where locals send and receive mail. It's the hub of the neighborhood, a Hell's Kitchen institution. It's the first place I went to the morning of 9/11. It may, in fact, be the last of the Mohicans.

People really talk at my pub and, get this, people really

listen. A think tank with beer mugs, my pub is the meeting place for a group of motley prevaricators I lovingly refer to as the Retarded Algonquin Round Table. Archie Bunker holds court there, sitting in the same seat every day without fail. As they say, I'd rather be with those people than the finest people on this planet.

The diversity of attendees at this institution is nothing short of inspiring. Doesn't that sound like a college catalogue? What I mean to say is, just about everybody and his brother drinks there. Wall Street execs, retirees, young, old, ex-military, Westies, union stagehands, Olympian drinkers, degenerate gamblers, a physician here and there, you name it. I don't want to get too specific here, as just about everybody and his brother might not care to be included in this hall of fame. Suffice it to say, the crowd is eclectic and electric. Politics are bandied about. Insane politics (as if there was any other kind). Barstool diplomacy is practiced on a quotidian schedule. Translation: an exaggerated and ludicrous response to any problem, with overwhelming and inordinate military force, e.g., carpet bombing and nuking. The suggested response to any international situation? Level 'em and/or make a parking lot out of the country. "Give peace a chance" is a refrain you'll never hear.

A bond formed in the neighborhood pub is a bond that knows no equal. Once you've been accepted as a regular and enjoy that status, you become a member of a family. Dysfunctional, albeit, but a family. Regulars receive birthday cards covered in alcohol-soaked scribbles of vague wishes and illegible salutations. And yet, you may know someone for twenty years only as Tommy Boy. Come to think of it, regulars have no last name. This should not surprise you coming from a guy named Lionel.

I've been to countless wakes and memorials for the dearly departed regulars of my pub. Someday Tommy Boy will go to mine.

But enough of this sudsy sentiment. There are rules to the bar: regulations, conventions, expectations, policies, protocols, proprieties, manners, and etiquette. Just as you can't play Monopoly without knowing that you'll get $200 for passing "GO," you can't play at the neighborhood pub without knowing that there are certain rules for passing through its doors. Namely:

+ **Drinking is NOT about getting drunk.** If you're drunk, you've lost the game. Now, you can be "overserved," which is a subtle distinction. Being overserved is a state which comes about when a demanding publican fails to gauge your impending inebriety and you accede to his plyings out of courtesy. In other words, you've had too much. But it's not your fault. You were excessively presented with hootch. The same thing happens at fast-food joints when the fourteen-year-old behind the counter suggests you super-size your extra value meal. As we used to say in the seventies, *it's the system, man . . . the system.*

+ **Never do shots.** This is for the college frat brat. Drinking is slow and deliberate. It's a marathon, not the hundred-yard dash.

+ **Never go to any bar with a velvet rope or a long queue of potential tipplers.** This is not a bar that you want to go to.

+ **Never go to a bar with a cover or a minimum.** This is not a bar.

+ **A bar doesn't have a live band,** though Irish bars on St. Paddy's day will have the requisite bagpipe ensemble and will play that tortuous dirge "Danny Boy." But not too much.

+ **Buying rounds for people? Think about it.** Is this a precedent you want to set?

+ **Always buy anyone a drink who bought you one.**

+ **Never drink anything whose name is not self-explanatory.** Name brand beer will suffice. (You can't doll up beer.) The name of the drink must convey the contents of the glass, not sound like something you'd pay for on cable. Chivas on the rocks (my favorite), also referred to as Vitamin C. Stoli and tonic. Rum and Coke. Get it? No Sex on the Beach, Fuzzy Nipple,

Screaming Orgasm. Nah! That's OK at a Bennigan's in the mall. But you should never hear those effete drinks ordered at a bar.

+ **No man will drink wine at a bar.** Sorry, oenophiles.

+ **Never order two different drinks in succession.** Never. Switching from beer to liquor is just fine—that's called tactical escalation. But once you've selected your liquor, stick with it.

+ **Never, ever, order a drink with a parasol, sparkler, or anything resembling patio furniture.** Fruit should be kept to a minimum.

+ **No man will drink a mojito.** (Remember: It's not self-explanatory.) No real bar will serve one.

+ **Women are lousy drinkers and must be watched carefully.** Their metabolisms are such that alcohol assimilates poorly. Not only that, they often eat poorly which fails to activate the pylorus, whereupon absorption is enhanced. Eat, ladies!

+ **Women should never yell "WOO!" for any reason.** Whether their favorite song is on the jukebox or some inexplicable feeling of oneness pours over them. Never yell "WOO!" or any of its derivative yells, yelps, and/or hoots.

+ **Men should avoid any unnecessary hugging and male bonding whilst imbibing.**

+ **Jukeboxes and music in general should always be played at a low level.** Drunkenness is associated with alcohol-induced deafness.

+ **Once gooned, people loose their sense of rhythm, rhythm which they most probably never had.** Therefore, Gene Krupa, no drumming on bars.

+ **As Cicero repeatedly stated, "No sane man will dance."** Never dance in a bar. Ever. Your sexuality will be called into question.

LIONEL LAW: Whilst getting waxed, never call a significant other, or anyone whose opinion you cherish. Cell phones should have alcohol meters on them that become disabled when they detect a BAC (blood alcohol concentration) of 0.09% or higher. (911 calls should always be allowed.) Note to Verizon. On a similar note, never leave a voice message on anyone's phone or answering machine when throwing one back. Period. You may be sober the next day, but your soused harangue will live on in perpetuity.

+ **"The girls get prettier at closing time."** "I went to bed with a 10 at 2 and woke up with a 2 at 10." These aren't just cute country tunes, these are the sad but true observations of the very wise. Scotch goggles exist. Ethyl alcohol can cause a temporary myopia that will transform a mouth-breathing troll into _____ (your hot babe here).

✦ **Barkeeps and publicans should remember that every sot traversing their portals is there to give them money.** Treat patrons with respect. Sure, have your boundaries and toss the occasional inebriate when his behavior is untoward. But be careful with banning, barring, and banishing. Remember, bars are not private clubs (see "public house" above), so watch it, Mr. High-and-Mighty bartender.

✦ **Buybacks should be customary at a 1:3 ratio,** i.e., one drink on the house after the third bought. Buybacks are to be expected from publicans, especially for regulars.

✦ **Time slips by.** *Tempus fugit* was coined in a bar. Watch the clock.

✦ **Never sing along or sing period in a bar.**

✦ **No barkeep should ever tell anyone calling via telephone for you that you're there or are to be expected.** They don't know you. I once had a novice bartender tell someone on the phone that I wasn't there *yet*. Needless to say, we had words.

✦ **Think long and hard about bringing a prospective girlfriend to your place.** If the arrangement sours, she's now got a place to harass you. Trust me on this one.

✦ **Beware of the unscrupulous barkeep.** Example: The owner buys you a drink (cf. "buyback") and instructs the cat behind the stick to give you one. He does, but you find it on your tab later. You're too whacked to read small print or enter into a dispute, so you pay it. Here's the solution. Keep track of your drinks with swizzle sticks. And at the end of the night, sell them back. (That was a joke.)

+ **This is a tad shady, but it works.** Know how to con a freebie or two. Here goes. When you're at your penultimate drink or two, pay the tab and settle up. Then while in conversation with your mixologist, ask for a "wee splash." Translation: not a whole, full drink, just a smidgen, a drop. Invariably, your host will give you what amounts to a full drink, especially if you've tipped him well. Asking him to "top this off" is not the same. That's another full drink.

+ **As for tipping, forget this nonsense about** *tip* **being an acronym for "to insure promptness."** That's nonsense. If this is your place and you frequent it often or want to, 20 percent or nothing. Period. Twenty percent, at least.

+ **Speaking of such, if you like a place from the onset, there's nothing wrong with tipping the barkeep from the outset.** No sweat. They'll love you. Remember, your bartender is the only thing standing between you and that glow.

+ **A note on swizzle sticks.** Strategically place used sticks in front of your drink, thus indicating to the barkeep when a buyback is in order. Three sticks = buyback. Tada!

Ignorance of the law is no defense. Neither is ignorance of the laws of tippling.

A NOTE ON DRINKING AND DRIVING.

Don't.

No, this isn't a public service announcement. It's just common sense. Don't drive after you drink. I know, I know: If drunk driving is wrong, why are there parking lots at bars? I've never gotten this one. How in the hell do they think you're getting home? Rickshaw?

Why is there happy hour? Ladies' night? Sink or swim? (God, I'm dating myself.) Dunno. Just don't drive.

And don't try to figure out when you can drive based upon your weight and consumption and the time. This is unadulterated bullshit. Inebriety and BAC are not subject to guesswork.

Look, this is the old prosecutor in me speaking. I prosecuted countless poor shmucks who never intended to commit a crime. BAC rises then falls. You may not be loaded when you start up your car, but may legally be fifteen minutes later.

Don't drive drunk.

Do not pass GO.

Do not collect $200.

Oh . . . and could you give me a wee splash?

THE GOD BRAIN

God created man in his own image.
Man, being a gentleman, returned the favor.

Got to love that Rousseau.

I'm not a doctor, and I don't play one on TV. Nevertheless I know that there's something in our human brain that lays the foundation for a God belief system. A God reflex. Something natural. Something hardwired. Some sort of genetic predisposition for both recognizing and creating God.

When a person professes a profound faith in God, a belief in some sort of spirituality, or a connection with something "bigger," things happen in the brain. Bear with me for a minute while I get all librarian on you. I'm going to refer to a book and it's not mine. Shhh. In *Why God Won't Go Away* (available wherever books, and personal hygiene products, are sold), authors Andrew Newberg, Eugene D'Aquili, and Vince Rause speak of neurotheology, a neodiscipline that tries to define the complex relationships between (perceived) spirituality and faith and the complex functions of the brain. And they know whereof they speak. Using high-tech imaging devices to peer into the brains of meditating Buddhists and Franciscan nuns, these guys discovered correlations between brain function and subjective religious experience.

This makes profound sense to me. Nothing can be experienced without a receptor site in the brain that allows for an appreciation of that feeling or concept. If you feel happy, sad, paranoid, or ambivalent, there must be a brain structure that is firing, allowing for those feelings. Much like taste buds that allow you to perceive sweet, there are "God buds" in the brain that permit, and I believe *cause*, your belief.

When people experience a heightened sense of spirituality it means that the brain is wired for that sense. That doesn't mean that God exists, but it may mean that a belief in God is a neurological illusion. (I can just see my grade school nun, Sister Mike Tyson, glaring at me for that observation.) When you feel the presence of God or something spiritual, when you appreciate that transcendental peace or equanimity, a portion of your brain is firing up to allow for it. (Much like the way the brain works when you eat chocolate, and I'm not kidding.)

Consider this. When we're faced with immediate peril, the brain acknowledges the danger because the initial input is real and there and true and actual. Doesn't matter what that danger is—could be a saber-toothed tiger, a burning building, or your ex-wife on hold. The important thing, here, however, is that the initial input is caused by an event, by something *real*. But what if the brain is able to "recognize" something that isn't real, something that isn't accompanied by an external stimulus? What if the brain can create a pseudoperception of something *it* created and didn't merely respond to? What if the brain, on its own, creates the sensation of something extant, something that is surreal, cosmic, supernatural, bigger than all of us? What if the brain creates God on its own?

We've seen this in psychiatric disorders. When someone stands on a corner alone yelling "Who ordered the veal cutlet?" we attribute that to schizophrenia or some psychotic fugue. To the person howling on the corner, however, that illusion, hallucination, or delusion is very real. The brain, perhaps in conjunction with some neurochemical disorder, registered something that wasn't there. To many, no, most, their belief in God is also very real. It happens all the time. I submit that people's supposed love of sushi and the ability to endure Yanni are likewise tricks of the brain.

This event happens with incredible frequency in religion and mysticism. I believe that there is a natural reflex that the brain is more than happy to produce that gives us humans a false positive for the existence of God and that sense of spirituality. How else could you explain why so many of us believe in a God when there is absolutely no evidence save anecdotal mythology and the occasional vision of the Virgin Mary on a grilled cheese sandwich?

Consider this: Statistics show that an overwhelming number of Americans believe in a God. Ninety percent of all adult Americans, if a 2003 Harris poll is to be believed. OK. Here's where it gets nice and circular: They see that fact as proof of God's existence. I don't get it. That's like saying that if four out of five dentists recommend Trident, then 90 percent of us can't be wrong and there must be a God.

When you take into consideration our uncanny ability to spot patterns and trends, the idea of a higher power helps to make things make more sense. Since the beginning of time, when man tried to figure out lightning, floods, and life itself, having a big invisible God in the sky pulling the strings made things make sense. It provided a locus of control; it gave order to the mess of life. A narrative. A story. A reason for being here. I get it. Not only is God hard-wired in us all, but the idea of an all-powerful God provides solace and comfort against the instability and unpredictability of life. If there's a God, we're not alone. He's calling the shots. Don't look at me; he's responsible.

Humans believe because they are human. God is created

naturally by the brain. God is an illusion, albeit a positive one, that the brain has conjured up. It's an absolutely perfect analogue to psychotic dementia and schizophrenia. But this psychosis is lauded and applauded. It happens to inspire good on occasion, maybe even beneficence. (Which is not, as some people think, a soluble fiber.) This psychosis gets people elected and is welcomed by all positively. Talk to an imaginary fairy and you're psychotic; talk to God and you're of faith.

I've read of neuroscientists who've mapped just where the God perception occurs in the brain. They've also tinkered with transcranial electromagnetic stimulation in an attempt to artificially recreate what the brain itself artificially creates—God. If this is ever perfected, the implications will be heard 'round the world. Atheists will announce a collective "A-ha!" Devout theists would object to the notion that God was and could be artificially induced and hence not real. Think more. If this was possible, could that brain site be zapped to give one a God "tune-up"? What if a retired Catholic like me could go in and have the God portion of my brain jump-started? I can see it now, Catholic schools trading catechism for jumper cables.

I'll go a step further: Not only is the God illusion and reflex subject to artificial manipulation (potentially), but romantic love—which, if you think about it, is an OCD analogue—is likewise fine-tunable.

I've no basis for this, but I think my hunch will be proven true.

I firmly believe, albeit as a layman, that our fascinating brain has within it a part that creates and manufactures *sua sponte* the Almighty. For how could you explain how humans since time immemorial have created this fantastic superstructure? How else can you explain Kelly Ripa?

To believe in God is human.

To be human is to believe in God.

INSPECTOR GADGET

Upgrade!

We all want the new gadget.

We must have it.

We must have the one that's smaller, pinker, and, oh yes, cooler. Who cares that a cell phone is so small it has to be repeatedly slid from ear to mouth like a bad imitation of Toots Thielemans. There's no interest in utility or practicality. Cell phones can only get so small before they become unusable trinkets. I've got a Web browser on my BlackBerry. With a screen the size of a Junior Mint. I can't see the screen! Hello!

Look, we all dug Maxwell Smart and the shoe phone, but he didn't prefer that mode of communication. Yeah, it was cool, but believe you me 86 didn't love pressing smelly shoe leather to his mouth just to make a call. I even heard the suggestion that one day cell phones will be implanted in our teeth. Teeth. I've got something to say to the genius who came up with that idea: What about a wrong number at three in the morning?

Let's talk about those obnoxious Bluetooth users. You know in their heart of hearts they think they're so cool. Look at me. A contraption clipped to my ear that signals to the world "If you had any doubt I was an asshole, here's Exhibit A." And, better yet, the latter-day ear trumpet that's affixed to one's ear, it's a transmitter and receiver of various wavelengths of radiation NEXT TO YOUR BRAIN! Now, you watch. I'll bet you that within twenty years huge, cauliflower-sized tumors growing out of our heads will be all the rage. It will be a sign of status. Like a trumpeter's lip, a hockey player's missing teeth, a wrestler's cauliflower ear.

And watch. Not missing a beat, Verizon will develop the TUMORFONE.

LIONEL LAW: If you are a man, no sandals. All right, all right, a few exceptions. Trappist monks and the Dalai Lama, fine. And if you get a gig in a Passion play, you get a pass.

BE AFRAID. BE VERY AFRAID.

My parents might have been possessed with a divine and supernatural erudition that I understand only now. Or maybe they were laboring under an advanced pre-psychosis that I've just traited upon. Or perhaps they were sadists. Whatever the cause, they make me laugh now, their warnings and chestnuts, those proscriptions and admonitions that scared the bejesus out of me. Here's my list—no doubt you have one of your own:

+ **You'll poke your eye(s) out.** Show me a kid who's never heard this and I'll show you an aardvark. I've searched high and low for anyone who lost her eye after failing to take heed of her parent's warning. A poked-out eye? I never met anyone who had this happen, but I wonder.

+ **You'll break your neck.** Oddly enough, it's not the broken neck that kills you but the asphyxiation that normally precedes any hypoxia via ligature. I just thought I'd clear that up.

+ **Don't run with scissors.** Why scissors? Why not a scythe or a butcher's knife or a pair of pinking shears?

+ **Your eyes will get stuck like that.** I've always had the ability to cross an eye. My right. I mean cross it. Think Ben Turpin, Marty Feldman. It's a gift. It allows me to mock the blind. (Not to worry, they never see it.) My mother swears that if you do this as a kid, your eyes will stick. Well, Mom, so far, so good.

+ **Your face will stay like that.** This one was in fact correct.

+ **Keep away from the dry-cleaning bags.** This was my father's favorite fear. He read once on the side of a dry-cleaning shroud that these dastardly sheets could and would lead to senseless suffocation. For reasons I can't begin to fathom, he took the "keep out of the reach of children" warning way past its limits. That is to say, that these bags had not just a life of their own, but sinister motives too. My father believed that these bags could move and slither and deprive life from the unsuspecting by enwrapping themselves around the mouths of innocents. (Like the myth of cats suffocating infants.) They had to be crumpled and smashed, their bloodlust quashed. They scare me to this day.

+ **Money doesn't grow on trees.** Self-explanatory but no truer words were ever spoken.

+ **Don't leave wet towels on the bed.** Wet equals damp. Damp leads to mildew. Mildew to bedspread funk. Besides, why not hang towels up after use? They were clean before they sopped up a supposedly clean body (orifices and body cavities notwithstanding). Certainly they were good for more than one use. After all, money doesn't grow on trees. See *supra*.

+ **I don't have stock in ___ (name your power provider).** We as children were power hogs eons before the specter of global warming and carbon footprints.

+ **Close the shower curtain.** The dreaded mildew monster strikes again. This omnipresent bacterial sniper was ready to knock us off whilst in the latrine grassy knoll. Mildew, how I hate the name to this day. Mildew? Wasn't she a guest on *Jerry Springer*?

+ **Don't stare at the refrigerator.** He was ahead of his time, my old man. Why open a refrigerator and stare at the contents within all the while letting cold air escape? Al Gore, eat your heart out. But how, you might ask, would one stare at the contents of the fridge without opening its door and letting the sacred cool air out? Telepathy? X-ray vision? I never found the answer to this question.

+ **When I was your age.** This is a phrase that I loathed as a kid but say constantly to everybody now, even those older than me. (Now that's fun!) It provides a sense of pseudowisdom and sapience. It can also be used along with "When I was in the Gulag" and is often accompanied with some sort of weather report, as in "When I was your age I had to walk twelve miles to school in the driving snow. Backwards, and without shoes."

+ **You can't go swimming __ minutes after eating.** My father swore that after consuming victuals, swimming would necessitate movement that would be impossible because of . . . something. Some visceral redirection of blood flow that would disallow extremities to move rhythmically as in, say, swimming. Where he got this, who knows. Every parent knows this and has sworn to repeat it.

+ **If you don't stop that, you'll go blind.** Blind? Nah! Hard to type? Well . . .

+ **Don't say what I think you're going to say.** My mother came up with this beaut. Read it again. What will you say? How does she know what you will say? And why not say it? Brilliant.

TRUST ME ON THIS

You're at a bar. A guy you know comes in. He comes in with a woman.

Never assume said woman is his wife.

Never acknowledge him until he initiates it.

I don't care if you've seen pictures of his wife.

I don't care if you were the best man at their wedding.

I don't care if their firstborn is named after you.

If the guy wants to be noticed, he'll let you know. Acknowledging him à la Norm in *Cheers* implies that he's a regular. Translation: A drunk. I shan't—yes, *shan't*—forget a regular who assumed that another regular entered with his wife. She wasn't. Bad news, kiddo.

Just imagine that interaction. (Speaking of assumptions, never congratulate an obviously pregnant woman on and for her life to be.)

Trust me.

DEATH AND TEXAS

Death is the best part of life. Why do you think they save it for the end?

I have no idea who said that, but it wasn't me.

Can you believe the syrupy nonsense that is associated with death? It's as if the grim reaper worked for Hershey. Here's one: I have awakened from the dream of life. Such unmitigated horseshit. Here's another: He's gone to a better place. A better place? Better than what . . . Des Moines? And how about this one: He's at peace. So is a rock. She's not suffering anymore. Nor is she enjoying anything.

I've been to the funerals of countless Sicilian relatives and I've heard it all. Every stupid comment about death and being dead. You wanna hear more?

He looks so natural. Right. He's had every ounce of blood

drained from him. This thing called a trocar was jammed into his gut and every organ of note was turned to mush, allowing for orangey chemicals to perfuse what's left of him. Orangey to mimic the color of life. Cotton's shoved up his ass and a number 9 pancake has been spackled over his rigor-mortised face. There's no back to his suit and, oh yeah, HE'S DEAD! And if this looks natural, what was he before? Grandpa Munster?

Humans love this death biz and have created mechanisms just to avoid the obvious: we die, we cease, we are no more. We are dead. Deceased. Departed. Lifeless. Gone. We will memorialize any thing or body. Have you ever seen a pet cemetery? Don't get me started.

No one wants to confront death as it is. Why not make stuff up? So we do. All of us. When we're afraid we make things up. We create a religion, a belief system, you name it. Reincarnation, Heaven, Nirvana. The Resurrection. Transcendental whatever. Anything to not address the fact that, as far as anyone can tell and as far as we've heard from those who've died, there is nothing to death but the cosmic POOF!

So obsessed are we with the notion that there's something after death that we watch television shows where mediums and soothsayers and charlatans swear that they talk to our beloved friends and family members who've "crossed over." Crossed over?! As if we're talking about the George

Washington Bridge and death is just the toll. Sorry, but we're talking about crossing over into decomposition and demate-rialization. Ashes to ashes and all that. Dust to dust. And then there's that soul thing. Our soul lives on. Or so the dead talkers claim. Funny, when they speak to our dead forbears, they never hear where Uncle Wally hid his money or who killed Aunt Sara. You've heard the stories before. The dead reassure us they're OK. I think the last thing about being dead is being OK. It's as non-OK as you can be. They're so incredibly man-made, these perceptions. Frank Capra couldn't do better. Let's face it, we've only heard from the "near-dead" and the operative word is "near."

Death is not an *oops*; it's not a mistake. It's inevitable. Predictable. Unavoidable. To be expected. Dead certain. And just as death is certain, it will also be certified, as in a death certificate. (This will come as good news for those of us who never received our high school diplomas. Something to frame at last.) Oh . . . and it will also be categorized. There are four types: natural, accidental, homicide, or suicide. That's it. Four possibilities of the inevitable. When some guy is exe-cuted, what is the cause of death? Homicide. Death at the hand of man. But if a four-pack-a-day smoker dies, what's that? Suicide? And what's an accident, anyway? If you run into a tree while skiing, is that an accident? Or is that the result of something stupid, say, skiing at a level you're not able to handle?

You'll note, however, that "near death" (you know, the tunnel of light and all that) isn't included in our group of four. Picture this: There you are dead or dying. Your family is gathered around your hospital bed. Or crime scene. Your children are crying for Mommy. A shining, warm tunnel of light beckons you to leave the world as you know it and go home. Go elsewhere. Unshackle that which tethers you to life. Leave this mooring. Something is calling you home. (Cue the angelic music.) But, oddly enough, you're given a choice. Give in to the warm bath of light and ostensibly God where all your lottery numbers are winners, where all your across-the-bar gazes are fruitful, or acquiesce to the entreaties of your young children who cry for your return. You, of course, return to the bonds of Earth. And why not, because if you didn't we'd never hear the story. You'd be *really* dead and not merely *near*. Even Larry King can't book that guest.

Sound familiar?

It is.

It's the so very human wishes of the so very humans who are so very afraid of the so very real death. We romanticize our crossing over. We perpetuate the myth that death is but traversing that border—flash our E-Z Pass and off we go to the next stage where a new, heightened reality is waiting. (Not to mention a nice, cold beer.) Going to that place where all is peaceful and tranquil, equanimity will abound. OK, maybe the harps and angels bit was far-fetched, but it shows that there's something to the hereafter. Right? Wouldn't it be nice, as Brian Wilson intoned?

Here's what I think.

The fact that so many people claim that they recall that magical light drift means that it's something that normally and regularly approaches what we believe to be near death. Let's be fair. There's always the account of the emergency room physician who's applied a series of cardiac jump-starts to what seemed to be no avail. There's the story of how the poor cadaver-to-be flatlined. They called a code. Yada yada. But miraculously(!) the stiff-in-waiting was revived. Voila! Life redux. But wait, this stinks, er, smacks of an explanation. Let's see.

Try this on for size: The patient was suffering from oxygen deprivation. Anoxia? Hypoxia? Pick your poison. Deprived of oxygen, the brain responded to said anoxia or hypoxia accordingly and in what may be the vestiges of memory the light scheme was perceived or maybe remembered. The fact that so many people experience the same thing indicates that it's a physiological response. Like sleeping or farting or watching reality TV. It does not, however, mean that there's a heaven that welcomes its new members with the light shtick.

And there you have it. A boring and simple explanation from an amateur of something that we'd prefer to see as musical and God-beckoning. That's what death is: boring and simple. But we humans can't take that for an answer. Whether we're Egyptians wrapping up King Tutandfuck or Houdini acolytes holding a séance, we just can't fathom the idea that that's that. Over and out.

Look at our funeral processes. That's the sickest thing that we still do. Next to NASCAR.

Dig. Grammy kicks and is carted away to be pumped with formaldehyde and a witch's brew of toxins that would scare the hardest-hearted New Jerseyite. All dressed up and no place to go. You know the routine. You file past the stiff and invariably some old-timer in the group marvels at how natural this stiff looks. Like they're sleeping. Yeah, they're sleeping all right. Really sleeping.

When I was a kid I went to countless wakes and funerals because the number of my relatives who died was, well, countless. Once I saw some casket-dweller wearing glasses. Glasses! I asked innocently why such was such and an aunt explained that Uncle Joe always wore glasses. This way people would recognize him. He never wore glasses to sleep. Does the fact that we're all here and his name is on the funeral home viewing room give the morbid death groupies a hint? Yeah, Uncle Joe always wore glasses . . . and breathed.

That's the insanity of death.

It's a macabre dance that we do-si-do to convince ourselves that this is just an untimely interruption. Uncle Joe will be back . . . after this commercial break.

And why do we bury the dead? We're an astral people

when it comes to God. We always look up to the heavens, God's house. Fertility religions believe that God's in the ground. They bury. Astral folks cremate so that the smoke will carry the soul UP to God. We've got it bass ackwards.

No, it kills us that we die. The idea of an absolute screeching halt to existence annoys us to no end. So what do we do? We pretend as usual. We manufacture all types of scientific analogues. The soul lives on. Conservation of energy. A transmutation of the spirit. The evaporation of the soul and condensation of the heart: a distillation metaphor. Death is just a life still—boil 'em up and bottle them for the hereafter. Funeral directors are life bootleggers.

And what about these poor bastards whose every waking moment is the sale and presentation of death? Remember when they were called undertakers? I don't either, as a matter of fact. Morticians came thereafter. Now they're funeral directors. In the future, we'll have thanaticians (from Greek mythology's *Thanatos*).

Plain and simple, there is simply no evidence that anything happens after death that we can either appreciate or want to know. We pray that somehow we'll be aware of our nonlife and will be able to communicate with our loved ones. We hope that we can talk with our dearly departed. It boggles our limited mind, the proposition that cognition and sense both come to a halt. That we are void, null. I certainly can't prove that we're otherwise. But why give in to this preternatural reflex?

Think of death as a sentence that stops suddenly before one can

---

LIONEL LAW: There exists an inverse proportionality between the size of one's lapel flag pin and his intelligence.

LAWN BOY

As a stupid and bored kid I was fascinated by the lawn mower. My dad's Toro. I loved the smell of the gas and the steam after he'd shower a hot, freshly fired mower with a garden hose to "cool it off." This Toro was unbelievable. Indestructible. Unmeltable. Metal heated to 12,000°F then cooled to 30K in an instant. A metallurgist's nightmare. I watched him as a kid (I was the kid, mind you) and one day asked if I could try it. Mow, that is. Put me in, Coach. Here comes the genius. No, sorry, he'd apologize. You're not a man yet.

What?!

I was five. A man, I thought. Nope. Not yet. Later came eight, ten. Then on that day, thirty-five (but I jest), age eleven or something, he said proudly, "Son, today, you are a man."

Understand that, prior to this great day, he let me push a toy mower behind him. Sure, kid, enjoy the fumes, but not the power, the *manhood* of pushing this grass-shearing machine. Not being Jewish, I never had the pleasure and honor of a bar mitzvah, so the *Toro* was my rite of passage.

The day had arrived.

I stood behind the mighty machine and within five steps realized that I'd been had. It sucked. To high heaven it sucked. What had previously been the perfume of gasoline was now the belching, noxious exhaust of this most inefficient plow. I pushed this inert thresher. In the hot August sun. In the hot, August, FLORIDA sun. I inhaled each petro-toxic belch of this contraption that I had marveled over. How fucking stupid was I?

I'd been had indeed. After, oh, twelve minutes I asked my father, who was unable to hide the look of "gotcha," why my sister, two years my junior, hadn't been exposed to this milestone. He responded without hesitation, "She's developing."

Developing?

Developing what? I've just grown an additional testicle, not to mention the hematoblast in my scrotum, from pushing this sled. What could she possibly be developing? I never found out and continued to mow my parents' lawn for years to come. As of today, I hereby swear, unto you and God almighty, I will never mow another lawn again.

Parents are cruel. Yet clever. My dad was the perfect

analogue to the drug dealer on the corner. Get 'em addicted by the allure of the suggestion of mower euphoria or whatever. Wanna get a population—or a son—hooked on anything? Tell him he can't have it.

Yet.

SEXUAL DYSLEXIA—DYSEXIA

Fellas, think you know everything there is to know about women and sex? You haven't a clue. Here's some higher education. Read this carefully. At least twice.

First, a woman's sexual apparatus, the incredible clitoris, makes the penis look like a little tail (its Latin translation). The hypersensate woman is blessed with an appendage that pound for pound, inch for inch dwarfs the penis in sensitivity. God blessed her with a sexual system that is electrochemical. Men's penises work on a system of hydraulics that requires reloading, with a limited number of firings. If a man enjoyed multiple orgasms at the rate of some women, he'd die of prostatitis and would most probably be found by a relative or neighbor curled up in a fetal ball like a bug singed over a match. Women are blessed beyond belief. They can diddle themselves whilst doing anything without the necessity of a damask or quicker picker-upper. If I were a woman, I'd never leave the house. Nature certainly preferred them when they were blessed in this special way.

Second, a woman is absolutely incapable of a completely detached one-night stand. It happens, don't get me wrong. They don't prefer it but will bend the rules occasionally. And don't believe all you see in that *Sex and the City* horseshit. Women are indeed open-minded and dare I say liberated. And they should enjoy the same dating behaviors that we do. But no man should ever fall for the crazy notion that a woman is "cool" with a man boinking others as well. When you dip your wick, men, something happens to a woman's head and heart. I don't care how old they are, how experienced, or how many times married. When a woman feels "used" it's curtains for you, Cochise. In fact, while we're on the subject, whenever I hear about abstinence programs in schools and finally stop laughing over the notion of *teaching* abstinence (Chapter 1: Don't Do It; Chapter 2: I Said Don't Do It, and so on), I suggest that young people should not have sex too early for precisely this reason. A young woman's heart and emotions may become scarred over the notion of being used and discarded. That's what should be taught in schools to kids, not the nonsense that condoms don't work and whatever else is taught in an abstinence class.

Finally, as to straying in relationships, women will have

sex for love; men will say they're in love for sex. It's as old as dirt and speaks volumes, again, as to the differences in us: the sophisticated and higher-order woman seeking a higher-order emotion, whilst the man trundles about thinking he can outsmart a woman with amorous bullshit. It takes two to tango, true, but she's a far more sophisticated dancer.

I'D LIKE TO BUY A VOWEL, PLEASE

I asked my mother what she wanted for her birthday once and she said, "A new son." That was a joke. No, she said she wanted a dictionary. A really good dictionary. A big, thorough, unabridged dictionary. A list of all our words with their exact meanings.

When I told my friends that my mother wanted a dictionary for her birthday they looked at me quizzically. A dictionary? A book with no plot or pictures, just a long list of words that nobody ever uses, like olefin, gillie, lagomorph, and democracy? Why a book of words? After all, they knew all the words, right?

That spoke volumes (not just as a blatant pun, you see) about the way we look at our language. We'll go to gyms and cross-train and do Pilates and yoga. We'll contort ourselves just to improve strength or endurance or to lose weight. But virtually everyone thinks that after a certain age, say, twelve, every word worth knowing is already known. And in a sense they're right. Think of when you were a kid and your mother pointed to her nose and you said "nose." That's what most people think of as a decent, well-rounded vocabulary. Can you describe the basest of things? Can you ask for directions, order food? Remember, we seek the bare minimum. That requisite collection of words that allows us to get by. The forty-third President of this great land said it perfectly.

> To those of you who received honors, awards and distinctions, I say well done. And to the C students, I say: You, too, can be president of the United States.
>
> —*(at a Yale speech, 2001)*

Anything more is showing off.

Showing off, as we all know, is fine if you're talking about boobs or brawn, but not, apparently, brains. The notion of showing off, or bragging, implies that you're boastful or arrogant without a basis for it. I'm sorry, if you can do something well, and you display it, that's not boastful, arrogant, or brash. It's been said a gazillion times, it ain't bragging if you can do it. To think that someone would be embarrassed for knowing something. For having a greater word palette. This is yet another example of the anti-intellectualism that so pervades our culture. It's hip to be stupid. It's not hip to be smart. *Beavis and Butt-head. Legally Blonde.* Spicoli. George W. Bush.

It seems that Americans don't find any fascination in knowing new words, in being able to explicate better, to describe more fluidly. I can't fathom why someone wouldn't want to be better able to describe something, to explain, to complain. It's incredible that the default American is satisfied with just barely 'splaining or communicating. We denigrate knowledge. We hate "big words." We roll our eyes at the sesquipedalian. When it comes to our distrust of those who can speak well, one word comes to mind: floccinaucinihilipilification.

The more words you know, the better you can communicate, the better a person you are. Wouldn't you want to be a logodaedalus? Wouldn't you love to know what a logodaedalus was? Well, get off your fat ass and look the word up. Feign curiosity, at least. What color would you mind not being able to identify or see? What sound or wavelength would you not want to be able to appreciate? Well, guess what, we can't change our hearing or vision. There's a certain range and field that we're stuck with. But you have the ability to add words and expression. So do it.

Wouldn't you love to put a Boeotian in his place deftly? Wouldn't you want to be able to craft a beautiful love letter to your wife? Or draft a letter to the editor about an issue that affects you and that you care passionately about? Words are free. That's right, absolutely free. They're powerful and give you the upper hand. It's a great way to bullshit your way through life. You can confuse with ease. You might just be blathering on, but it *sounds* good. It gives your adversary the impression that you know more than she does. It's a great way to exhibit panache.

And it's free.

FOOT SOLDIER

This is mean, priggish, and rude. Not only does it deal mostly with the female among us, it deals with a subject that most people don't even notice. But it bothers me to no end, and that's all that matters.

Feet.

Hideous feet exposed via the sandal, to be precise.

If you have ugly feet do not, repeat, do not wear sandals of any kind. Ever. You know what ugly means. Ugh. Yuck. Ouch.

If you have fetlocks instead of feet, skip the sandals.

If you have hooves instead of feet, skip the sandals.

If your feet are so malformed that it looks like you sleep on a perch, skip the sandals.

If the word *gnarled* comes to mind when describing your tootsies, abandon the thought of sandals altogether.

If you suffer from toebesity, a neologism denoting stubby toes (short, fat, mini-sausage, pigs-in-a blanket toes), no sandals.

If your peds are adorned with bunions, corns, and barnacles, if your toes are bent and/or twisted, if your hammers are located not in your toolbox, but on your feet, do not wear sandals. And don't even think about nail polish. Painting toenails merely calls attention to ugly feet, like slapping a coat of latex on a condemned building. Nobody's fooled. A layer of Ballet Slipper Pink doesn't cut it when what you really need is a sturdy pair of Wellington boots.

Cute shoes aren't cute if the foot that fills them is hideous. I am shocked—shocked! I say—when I pass a shoe store and see a woman holding up a sandal, marveling at its construction, ooh-ing and ah-ing at its architecture and design, yet completely overlooking the fact that her feet look like they belong to a Clydesdale. Women probably feel the same way when they see a man wearing a Speedo.

MISS AMERICA. I SURE DO.

The beauty pageant is the minstrel show of our time. It's a demeaning spectacle that serves no purpose other than to objectify women and perpetuate the idea that their worth is tied to their beauty, boobs, and bullshit. Now, granted, the minstrel show was performed by a bunch of white guys mocking black men with exaggerated features and the like (who thought that one up?). After a while, public consensus (and conscience) took over and decided that this act had to go. (What ever happened to the guy who would spin plates on a stick?) But what I don't get about Miss America is that it's women mocking women with exaggerated features and the like. (Okay, sometimes I do like.) But the point is . . . where's the uproar? From women? Barely a peep. Oh, a few here and there. But why is this relic of ideal womanhood still around? And whose ideal is it, anyway?

But I'm getting ahead of myself.

First let's look at the haughtiness and hilarity of what a *pageant* is. It's defined as an event with two components: an exhibition and a procession. What a beauty *pageant* is is a cattle call, a slave auction without the auction, wherein women are paraded across a stage all the while pretending that what they're showcasing and we're celebrating and acknowledging is talent, brains, and, oh yeah, beauty. Right. But wait. This just in: The *beauty* prefix has been dropped. They're now referred to as pageants. (And pimps are now called love brokers. Give me a break.)

What frosts my balls is when I'm accused by some of being, get this, misogynistic and sexist when I rail against a stupid public procession of young women vying to see who's the prettiest. How can women tolerate this unless it's actually something they aspire to? And don't give me that shit about talent or her views on world peace. The only "piece" the public is concerned with is . . . A beauty pageant is about the evening gown and swimsuit, and who are we kidding, it's the swimsuit. That's it. The other nonsense is like Hamburger Helper; it just spreads out the show. Hell, there should be a stripper pole for the "contestants." Better yet, how 'bout them picking up small change the hard way. (Sorry about that. Not a nice visual.) It's demeaning. It's anachronistic.

Please, a word about nude dancers. OK, I can't think of a word, but let me make something clear. I respect them far more than their pageant cousins. A pole dancer has no illusion of doing anything more than inspiring hard-ons. A lap dance and a pole slither are her only demonstrable talents. She speaks not of world peace or international relations. She most probably has a husband and a couple of kids and makes a shitload of money "dancing." Pageant tarts believe the facade they think they're creating and think we believe.

So long as there's the pageant, women will trail behind men socially and politically. It's the reminder that when all is said and done, a woman's look and shape are what's counted. You'll never see a pageant sponsored by Mensa. Sure, there are the Siemens (formerly Westinghouse) and other great science scholarships where women excel. Let's not forget those, but let's also not forget they're not covered on TV. Did you hear the latest? Guess who carried the 2008 Miss America Pageant? I shit you not, The Learning Channel.

There's no male counterpart to the beauty pageant, even for gay men. Musical theater doesn't count. Messrs. Universe and Olympia are about physique and steroids. There's no dinner jacket portion to that exhibition.

No, this is just sick no matter how you look at it. It's tolerated and, worse, aspired to by women. They're the culprits. No matter how I argue that these events perpetuate all that is wrong with society's image of women it is women who keep these things going. Oh, they'll argue that it's all about scholarships and the like, but who are we shitting? Come on. And women actually believe, or I hear many say, that men are the reasons for this. That men inspire this attention to looks and pulchritude. There's a big difference between appreciating something and encouraging obsession and body dysmorphic disorder. Men have long been the scapegoats for this insanity. Just look at a Victoria's Secret catalog if you have any doubts over the psychotic preoccupation with looks and sexiness.

We love to point to the Middle East to see the demeaning way that women are treated. They are forced to wear burkas in Afghanistan. They can't drive a car in Saudi Arabia (and they're not that swift here either). Women are executed if they're raped because they've dishonored their families. While we're not at this level, yet, we have our own superstitious bullshit that keeps hammering home the idea that when all is said and done, women are to be pretty. Just stand there with your store-bought tits, collagen lips, and Botoxed foreheads, your hair extensions and liposuction, tummy tuck and bleaching, fake nails and pierced you-name-it, and smile. That's it, smile, little lady, so we can give you the once-over. Turn around, honey, let's see the ass. OK, fine, now bounce offstage like the good little tart you are so we can see the next model. Oh, and can you give us your name and the state you, ahem, "represent." Not that we give a shit, mind you, who you are and where you're from but our original idea of having you tagged like cattle didn't go over so well with the sponsors, so we'll feign interest in your name and state.

The embodiment, the essence, the quintessence, epitome, you name it of this horseshit is Caitlin Upton. All right, I'm going to pretend that you don't know the name as I'm sure you've never heard of Typhoid Mary, Madame Curie, Margaret Mead, or Rula Lenska. I'll play along. Caitlin Upton was the 2007 Miss South Carolina Teen USA and she was vying for the crown of Miss Teen USA 2007. Miss Upton went on to place fourth.

As part of the pageant's desire to create the illusion that we gave a shit about what a kid thought about anything, she was asked a question. Now before we look at the question, consider the hilarious irony of this whole event. This "contestant" was asked a question about . . . drumroll . . . IGNORANCE. Rim shot. Here's the question:

"Recent polls have shown a fifth of Americans can't locate the U.S. on a world map. Why do you think this is?"

Now I don't want to quibble with the poll takers or their findings, but 20 percent can't find the U.S.?! Twenty percent of what, coma victims? And even with the North America thing and the Florida doohickey that sticks out, they couldn't approximate where their country was. Wow.

But back to Caitlin. OK, now here's the payoff. Caitlin thinks it over and provides this beaut heard round the world.

"I personally believe that U.S. Americans are unable to do so because, uh, some, people out there in our nation don't have maps and, uh, I believe that our, uh, education like such as, uh, South Africa and, uh, the Iraq, everywhere like such as, and, I believe that they should, our education over here in the U.S. should help the U.S., uh, or, uh, should help South Africa and should help the Iraq and the Asian countries, so we will be able to build up our future, for our [children]."

Now, I know what you're saying. Who cares? George Bush 43 was mentally retarded and came up with better doozies daily. (Remember how he understood those who want to put food on their families?) She's not even eighteen, bless her heart. And God knows if her parents pushed her or if she was medicated. She's just a kid. Right. Point well taken.

But what most have missed is that she's being asked anything in the first place. Caitlin Upton was not being paraded onstage as a possible cure for geographical ignorance. (I'm sure the cartography contingent of the Miss Teen USA crowd was disappointed.) This was merely an attempt to create the illusion that this cattle auction was something more than T&A. At least this beats the dreaded talent portion of the auction, er, pageant. Baton-twirling (great for a half-time show, but as a talent?), classical violin, and opera singing (the stern looks of sincerity crack me up everytime). A dramatic reading (translation: overacting). Dance (think a crazed-jazz rendition à la Laura Petrie in capris). Or something completely fucked up, a ventroliquist. Again all attempts to say, see, we care about things other than your accoutrements. Now let's see your ass, honey.

And the audacity of the names of these events floors me even more. Miss USA. OK. Miss America. Huh? North, South, or Central? Miss Universe. Miss World. Does Universe trump World? Is this to appease the pissed-off Venutian?

The list of Miss contests is staggering. There is no end to the items, vegetables, crops, and farm tools that pageants won't affix a "Miss" to—Miss Artichoke, Miss Intermediate Diesel Wheat Thresher. What next? Miss Benign Lipoma? Miss My Husband But My Aim is Improving? So long as a ceremonial sash denotes colorfully the Miss subject matter, no award or pulchritudinous paean is beneath the contestant.

Then there are the Mrs. Pageants for the longer-in-the-tooth mom set: women hanging on to the idea that they're still hot. Ladies, give it a rest. Let's add a new wrinkle (bad pun). It seems that pageant contestants today regularly spend colossal sums for plastic surgery, breast implants, liposuction, tanning, teeth-whitening, hair extensions, you name it. It's now part of the pageant. So this already unnatural event becomes even more unnatural by celebrating all that's not natural. At least in major-league sports, athletes are penalized for steroid use. Shouldn't there be a similar prohibition here? And isn't it troubling that the women who are having these procedures are, say, eighteen?

And let's not forget the little Miss pageants. Who will ever forget JonBenét Ramsey looking coquettish in those creepy pageant photos at, what, age four?! Don't tell me that this kid didn't have her hair bleached. This shit has no end. This is nothing more than beauty-obsessed women vicariously living off their kids. If I can't be pretty anymore, then goddammit my kid will. It's child abuse per se. Look, it's tough enough for a little girl to grow up normal in these times. And there are scores of royally messed up kids who became so after living relatively normal lives with normal messages. Just what is a child to believe when she's brainwashed and indoctrinated into a world that inspires such distortion? The idea, again, of a little girl made up and paraded about to look sexy is sick.

And we haven't even touched on cheerleaders, Playboy bunnies, Hooters gals. Look at me! I'm pretty! I'm sexy!

It's all sick.

And so, so sad.

THE SECOND (OR THIRD) LUCKIEST
MAN ON THE FACE OF THIS EARTH

This happened. Some time back I was asked to provide a play-by-play of sorts at Yankee Stadium. *The* Yankee Stadium. It seemed that George Steinbrenner, a Tampa denizen, very kindly gave permission for a charity softball game between the *CBS Evening News* and *Late Night with Conan O'Brien* to be played on that hallowed field. It was the least I could do.

There I was standing atop home plate in *the* most famous sports venue, next to the Sportatorium in Tampa. (Joke.) Inasmuch as this was a charity event I explained to the crowd that what I was about to do was in no way intended to be disrespectful, but that I had to do it.

As any vaguely sentient American cultural historian remembers, in 1939 Lou Gehrig stood at that very site and recited his courageous valedictory before a packed crowd. "Today, I consider myself the luckiest man on the face of this earth." Remember, it echoed as the sound wrapped around the stadium. *Today-ay-ay I consider myself-elf-elf.* Perhaps one of the most famous moments in all of American sports history. In 1942 Gary Cooper recreated the scene in *The Pride of the Yankees.*

So when I strode to home plate to begin announcing this charity event it hit me. There I was at home plate. Yankee Stadium. The House that Ruth Built. So, standing there with a mic, I in fact repeated that historic phrase and to my surprise that echo pattern does swirl around the stadium. I repeated that phrase after, as stating, apologizing beforehand. "Today, I consider myself the luckiest man on the face of this earth."

Now whether Cooper recreated that effect in Yankee Stadium or on a movie lot I don't know. And, OK, maybe it was the pitcher's mound and not home plate. Big deal. But if he didn't, *I* was the second person ever to utter those immortal words at Yankee Stadium, OK, from home plate, so what.

So if you're in a bar and you bet some fellow tippler who the *second* (OK, third) person was to ever utter those very words at Yankee Stadium, you can safely answer that I was. Either the second or third.

Top that.

KIDS TODAY

When I see kids today tooling about on their bikes with helmets, elbow and knee pads, Kevlar jumpsuits, and the like, it makes me sad. When I see kids armored more heavily than a Humvee I am particularly sad, because it speaks to me of the wussification of America. And that's not a good thing. What are they armored from?

Falling down?

Gravity?

Life?

What kid today knows the fun of owning a BB gun or, better yet, a pellet gun, a Crossman like I had? This was a miniaturized .22 caliber rifle. I mean a fucking RIFLE that could, but never seemed to, kill. The velocity of a pellet, which is the size of, oh, a bullet, shot from this baby was lethal. Oh, no, this would be considered unsafe today, something unsuitable even with parental supervision and a stern warning.

It seemed that we were impenetrable in my day. Elbow and knee pads?! I don't even remember training wheels. No self-respecting kid would be caught dead with helmets and pads and other safety devices. Hell, we'd be laughed off the playground. When we skateboarded and had an injury, say, a femur poking through shattered skin, Mom would spray the all-purpose Bactine and off we'd go. Infection? Nah, that's for girls.

We were fearless and maybe didn't know any better. We drank from hoses and used public restrooms and played outside until dark. There was no antibacterial soap or antibacterial anything. We didn't have nannies or learning specialists and we didn't call our parents every twenty minutes on our cell phones.

It was a better day.

One Christmas I received a wood-burning set. Translation: soldering iron. This thing would heat up to smelting temperatures and we'd, well, burn wood with it. Actually, the idea was that we'd adorn pieces of balsa with the singed imprints of this thing. I still have no idea of what the purpose of this was. The potential for injury was inordinate. But no one ever was hurt.

Kids in my day enjoyed Mattel's Creepy Crawler

Thingmaker which in essence was a hot plate that heated up to a skin-searing 300+ degrees wherein a toxic liquid goop was squirted into molds and heated up, thus making plastic bugs and critters. This would have been a product liability lawyer's wet dream, but, alas, no one was hurt so no one dared sue. After all, what do you expect when you give an eight-year-old a portable cauldron?

While we're on the subject of hot and potentially dangerous items, let's not forget fireworks. Living in Florida with the Carolinas not too far away, there was an unwritten rule that any kid in the neighborhood going anywhere near this fireworks capital would take orders for the real stuff. Honest to god fireworks. Translation: colorful dynamite. M-80's, Roman candles, bottle rockets with reports and color, and no one got hurt.

See, when a boy opens up a pack of Black Cats, and that shimmering gray silky gunpowder coats his fingers, it's almost erotic. Never satisfied with merely lighting one and running away like a pussy, he'd immediately combine bunches of them and affix them together. More bang, more danger. M-80's were the Dom Perignon of explosives, and make no mistake, they were explosives. These babies could shred any mailbox and wreak utter diabolical havoc. One particularly sick friend of mine decided that an additional harm factor could be added by lacquering one with glue and rolling it in

BB's for that shrapnel effect. Now that was living. Albeit with the occasional close call. How about attaching a fishing weight and firing it from a wrist-rocket, *the* slingshot of its time. Deliver this payload from above and you'd be sure to scatter a crowd. I can recall running with two Roman candles in each hand as they fired fiery phosphorous balls at some poor kid who, remarkably, was unscathed. Guess my aim was off.

And then there was the greatest potentially harmful item of them all: lawn darts. These were as stated darts, very *heavy* darts, with plastic fins (adding to their aerodynamic lethality) that would be thrown into the air for what reason I have no idea. Should one have landed on a hapless tike's head it would be curtains. These things could have impaled a steer skull. But no one got hurt, even at Halloween when we'd buy these costumes that came in a box with a plastic see-through cover. The box housed a chemically treated, combustible gown (or shroud, more appropriately) depicting your character. I was always the Devil while others were the benign-Disney-character type. Come to think of it, I was the Devil every single year. To this day, as a matter of fact.

If you were within a yard of an open flame, self-immolation was assured. You also had a mask that attached via an elastic strap and guaranteed no peripheral vision whatsoever. So off we'd go into the night with our napalm costume and sight-obscuring masks, hoping all the while that the car that would hit us would at least have the decency to screech its wheels as it ran us over. Blinded and flammable, that was Halloween.

And nobody was ever injured.

Much.

ADAM AND EVE:
CAN YOU SAY INBREEDING?

I realize you can't take biblical myths too seriously. They're parables, allegories, even syllogisms. The Bible is replete with all kinds of stuff and I'd rather discuss the legitimacy of professional wrestling than the Bible. And some of those stories are fun—the loaves and the fishes, the water into wine (my favorite). Jesus was great with food and vino, but couldn't he have cured cancer? Jesus Christ!

But I digress.

When it comes to Adam and Eve, people really do take it seriously. This beaut from Genesis (I and II, you pick) is the basis today for creationism, which is a pseudoscience in the truest sense. Pseudoscience is defined as theories or claims about the natural world that allege or appear to be scientific but are not. Think alchemy, astrology, *The New York Post*, intelligent design. In fact, it's more pseudo-pseudoism for it defies all that vaguely resembles logic.

So we are led to believe that after a period of nothing, the world was created and God created Adam and his paramour, Eve. (Remember, they were never married.) They were created from dirt and a rib. OK, fine. They were ostensibly created intact and never grew from infancy. Seems there was never a Lil' Adam or a Mini Eve. No Pampers, no preschool, no junior high, no prom. Fine. It also seems that A&E were created right around 4000 BCE, as some scholars have calculated. *Calculated.* Right. A&E were tossed from the Garden of Eden after Eve, in one of her moods, failed to adhere to dietary restrictions—their only rule to maintain their place in paradise. They then had Cain and Abel as their offspring and that oft-forgotten Seth. You know the story. Cain slays Abel. Now we're left with Adam, Eve, Cain and what's-his-name. Fine.

So I ask the all-important question: Where did the Koreans come from?

Now it would be fun to sit around and parse this fantastic tale and pick apart the myriad inconsistencies that contaminate this story. That's boring. I'd rather pick apart the story line of *Gilligan's Island*.

What is most fascinating here is that anyone actually, truly, honestly believes that this simple and innocent parable is anything more than a simple and innocent parable. How could any sentient human being pay the slightest attention to this poor man's excuse for mythology? George Lucas in a hallucinogenic mushroom cloud couldn't fathom this construction. Come on, it's not true. It's just a story. A story that has to begin somewhere.

I cringe when I hear people subscribe to the myth that evolution is up for debate. That not all scholars agree. Well, not all legit scholars. You have to have the IQ of a soap dish or a speed bump to question the absolute fact of evolution and believe in a creationist view of mankind and the universe. I hear it all the time. Evolution is just a "theory." Well so is gravity; it's also a fact. No one doubts the existence of gravity, but there have been very serious disagreements over the theory of how gravity, a fact, works. Whether the Newtonian version or Einstein's, it's still a fact. Stephen Jay Gould, God bless him, often reminded us that while the debate lingered objects didn't hang suspended in midair. Light is a fact. What theory best explains it? A wave theory? Particle? Quantum? Theories, Gould posited, are not the last rungs of the evidentiary ladder. Some hierarchical progression from fact to hunch to guess to the much-maligned theory. Theory explains fact. Theory can even explain theory. Enough with this! You're missing the point. Law versus theorem versus hypothesis, who gives a shit! Evolution is a fact and A&E is bullshit.

Science and religion *can* coexist in, as Gould suggested,

nonoverlapping magisteria. Two schools of thought that never intruded into each other, that abutted at best. You can believe in God and enjoy a concomitant belief in science. Perhaps science is, after all, the grammar of God's language. Popes Pius XII and John Paul II both endorsed the notion in two, count 'em, two encyclicals that a good Catholic could believe in evolution and still remain a good Catholic. The proviso was so long as you believed that the final product, man, was imbued with the spirit of God. Fine. I'll buy that. Kinda. Even they saw the sapience of understanding that the truly miraculous (or ostensibly such) has a mechanism to explain it.

Which leads to the idiotic proponents of intelligent design. In 1802, William Paley (the English theologian, not the CBS czar) wrote that if one were to find a pocket watch in a field, he wouldn't think that natural forces somehow acted in concert to construct this timepiece but that some superior intellect built it. Funny, I'd just think someone lost their pocket watch. But I digress. Ah, Paley: the Bill O'Reilly of his time. Utter nonsense.

But so goes this group of creationists who believe that the universe and evolution and the eye and DNA and, hell, NASCAR are so inexplicably complex and so far beyond the notion of a natural selection, a beautiful, perhaps God-"ordained" process.

Let me return to my reason for this screed. Simple minds

have construed the world's greatest novel, the Bible, as fact. No rational person, no one of rudimentary education, no person with a scintilla of common sense could possibly believe that. Adam & Eve?! Puh-leeze. And a disbelief in A&E in no wise vitiates the sagacity and goodness of the Bible *in toto*. Contract law provides for the doctrine of severability wherein a contract that contains an unenforceable clause is not *per se* invalid if that portion can be severed or expurgated. A disbelief in the scientific truth of A&E says nothing about the good word of the Sermon on the Mount and in no way abrogates the Book of Fellatio (my favorite).

For Chrissake people, wake up.

This is to inform you that some or all of your order has shipped.

(Just messing with you.)

I MUST HAVE PENIS

The Spanish accent is unique. Certain words and word forms prove difficult. Words that begin with the letter *s* followed by a consonant are pronounced with an *e* before the word. *Stop* becomes *estop*. (No estoppel jokes, please.) *Sleep* is pronounced *esleep*. Words that end in *ts* are pronounced minus the *t*. *Nuts* becomes *nuss*.

Got it?

Now here's what happened.

A friend of mine was getting married. I flew to the wedding with his mother, a lovely lady whose native language is Spanish with a Cuban accent and dialect. A lovely woman.

We flew to Minneapolis and then took a puddle jumper to the middle of nowhere in Wisconsin. The plane, as you can imagine, was quite small. Since this was pre–9/11, the pen. It was very tight, very

y, did it carry.

ated a few rows behind me. She

ed aloud if there would be any

man came down the aisle carrying

garbage bag filled with apples, crack-

lly first-class treatment.

er is far from loud but she could be eas-

ne in this tiny plane, what with the rum-

e engine that necessitated volume.

oung man, a pimply, Nordic-looking, carrot-

esotan-type kid whose name could easily be

ppy, came by our seats, my friend's mother

ple question in a very pronounced and easily

an accent.

tell you she's a lovely woman?

, here goes:

e dutiful Rusty stood there with his garbage bag filled

whatever and with a smile on his face asked if there was

ything he could get the lovely woman. Now, mind you,

's loud but you can hear everything anyone was saying.

What would the lady like? Her wish was Rusty's command.

Making sure the young lad could hear her request, she
inquired, "Do you have *penis*?"

Silence.

"I haven't had *penis* since Minneapolis."

More silence.

Rusty was red-faced.

Even the pilots could hear this and looked bac
woman demanding a phallus in seat 5A.

A penis?!

Quite a tall order for a commuter carrier. Rusty was
founded. Though he hadn't exactly inventoried all of the
bag's contents, he was pretty darn sure he was out of that
It must have crossed his mind that this might have bee
advance of sorts. This was hardly the scene for the mile I
club.

I had to do something.

I stood and announced, "Peanuts. She wants *peanuts*."

Exhalation was almost unanimous. A look of relief wa
seen on Rusty's face.

She had her peanuts and I have this story.

It's true. Swear to God.

HATE CRIMES:
CAN YOU SAY TAUTOLOGY?

Hate crimes. This has got to be one of the greatest redundancies in the history of our civilization. Hate crimes. And I hate them. Who can possibly be against hate crimes? What's the issue, you ask? You've heard about them; they're in the papers every day. A noose is found, a swastika painted, a cross burned. You know the story.

Hate crimes? As opposed to what—love crimes? Whatever happened to plain old crimes?

Hate- and bias-crime (*bias crime?!*) legislation is the product of a royally pissed off public, not too keen on having people dragged to death because they're black or virtually crucified and left to die because they're gay. I get it. I loathe the notion of a black family being terrified by a cross burning in their front yard. I am absolutely against such activities. No equivocation here. No jokes.

And yet, I have a problem with hate crimes.

A big problem.

Hate crimes were designed to mollify the constitutionally illiterate. Hate crimes punish people for their motivation in committing a crime. First, a crime, as you know, is an action that has incarceration as a possible penalty, no matter how remote the possibility of jail or prison is. While some offenses are punishable by civil penalty or fine, if incarceration is a possible punishment, it's a crime. Speeding tickets aren't crimes because they can only be punishable by fine or license suspension but not jail. Victim crimes are what we're talking about here. When someone hurts somebody else.

So, back to the hate crime.

The hate crime deals not just with the *what* of the crime, but the *why* and the *who*. That is to say, it singles out why a crime was committed and against whom. A person is selected as a victim because of his race, religion, whatever. Said person is the victim of a crime that would still be a crime if committed against anyone. But the *why* part is critical. The hate criminal punched the man because he was a Jew, he burned down the house because its owner was gay. The thought, the motivation, the reason—that's what's being singled out. That's what makes a crime a hate crime.

But note the operative word: crime. A crime that is already cognizable at law. A law that already proscribes a behavior, a behavior that is not only *not* protected by law, but is punishable by it.

Now remember also that hate speech is protected speech—unless you're a radio shock jock. (Protected from criminal prosecution, that is, not corporate anger. Drop an n-bomb. Go ahead. You can't be arrested for it but you sure as hell can be fired.) Anyway, back to our sponsor. There is no criminal statute that prohibits your calling anyone anything. You can call me an effeminate Mayan. You can call me a four-eyed dipsomaniac with fallen arches. You can even call me a Bush conservative. (No, wait, now you're pushing it.) Not only that, you're free to tell anyone what you think of their race, sexual orientation, or heritage. Calling someone a dirty mestizo, even if they're not dirty, is not against the law. It may be hateful speech but it's not hate speech; it's protected by the First Amendment. And that goes for the dreaded N-word, the C-word, you name it.

On the other hand, hit someone and you're subject to being arrested. That's the law. That's not speech. You know the old bromide, my freedom of speech ends at the tip of your nose. Hitting someone is assault and/or battery. It's clearly against the law.

But what if I were to hit you (against the law) and simultaneously state that you're a dirty mestizo (protected speech) and that was the motivation I had for hitting you? In some places, that would be a hate crime. Get it? Taking protected speech and coupling it with a crime that already exists is a hate crime. A hate crime, by the way, that zaps you extra hard because you're stupid enough to explain why you've committed a crime. (As of the time of writing, stupidity is not yet a crime.)

Go ahead, call someone a fag. Just don't hurt him at the same time. If you just hit him while remaining silent, it's probably a misdemeanor. Accuse him of being Paul Lynde *and* hit him, now it's a hate crime and probably a felony. Moral of the story: Keep your mouth shut.

The equation would look something like this: protected speech + law already on the books = hate crime. But it shouldn't, because it's patently unconstitutional and just plain wrong.

Still not sure about hate crimes? How about a love crime? Hit someone and simultaneously say you love them. (No Marv Albert jokes, please.) Will the statement of love mitigate your sentence? It shouldn't.

Motivation is irrelevant. What inspired you to commit a crime may be relevant at sentencing but shouldn't be used to aggravate the sentence of an existing crime. A sentencing judge should always take into account the particulars of a crime. Everyone's different. Take robbery, for example. The fellow who's caught robbing a store of baby formula and diapers may (and should) be sentenced differently than someone who takes beer and cigarettes. They're both the same crime, but a judge can look at mitigating facts and sentence accordingly. The same as the case of someone who terrorizes a family by burning a cross as opposed to someone who merely vandalizes property. (Does anyone remember toilet-papering homes? Thought not.)

If you were terrorized by an arsonist or assault committed against you, tell the judge at sentencing. Provide for such in a victim's impact statement. The degree of suffering a victim has endured is always relevant. No two robberies are the same. Just leave out the defendant's motivation. We should never care why a crime was committed or what the criminal was thinking during the commission of his crime. Sure, motivation is relevant insofar it can help prove intent, but it should never be the subject of a crime in and of itself.

Now let's also look at the confused hate and bias criminal. We all know that there are the usual symbols that are associated with certain examples of hate speech. Burning a cross on the lawn of a black family. Spray-painting swastikas on a Jewish temple. These acts are straight from the hate criminal's instruction manual. What about a not-so-swift hate criminal?

Say some jerk hasn't available wood to construct a cross that will be set aflame on a black family's property. He instead finds an old Christmas tree and incinerates it.

Assume *arguendo* another jerko spray paints Stars of David on a Jewish temple. What do these statements say?

What if it causes confusion and head scratching versus anger or fear? What if that's the hate criminal's version of a racial or anti-Semitic statement? Do those symbols count? Are they hateful if not immediately recognizable as standard hate speech messages? Dunno.

The underlying offenses are indeed crimes—trespass, criminal mischief, vandalism, perhaps even burglary.

And what if you call someone a fag, hit him, and he's not gay? Was that a hate crime? What if you burn a cross on the lawn of a white family? This is just insane. Not only must you know your epithets but the slur or hateful speech must be correctly used against a correct victim who is listed as being protected under the statute. Hate speech about race, gender, nationality, religion, or sexuality may be included in a statute prohibiting a hate crime. But derisive and hateful references to political affiliations may not be covered by statute nor may arcane nationalities. Attention, Aleuts! It's open season on you.

So what to do? Simple. Charge the miscreant with the crime(s) he's committed. Then when it comes to sentencing, let him have it. A judge can certainly take into consideration the effect on the victim. If a black family was terrorized by the act, break it off in him (an actual phrase I heard a judge utter once). Penalize the criminal consistent with the effects on the victim but not his motivation or thoughts and beliefs.

I recall a case I prosecuted. A home was torched because its owners were gay. Fine. (Well, not fine, but bear with me.)

We charged this arsonist with, get ready, ARSON! First degree arson, baby. The max. I was fighting fire with fire. But then I was approached by one of the owners, who demanded that I file the case as a hate crime. We had no specific hate-crime legislation covering arson at the time and I tried to explain this to the understandably pissed-off victim. Never mind that the defendant was charged with the maximum felony, punishable by up to thirty years in prison. The owner was relentless in demanding that it be prosecuted as a hate crime. It was in our vocabulary; it was in the news. HATE CRIMES.

What to do? What to do? Eureka! I simply announced to the sentencing judge that this was a hate crime. Tada! The victim wanted some kind of acknowledgment that this was a hate crime and, well, he got it.

Better yet, the jerkoff arsonist was maxed out, the victim was happy, and the judge took into consideration the effects on the victim/homeowner. The arsonist was punished for his *acts,* not his *motives.*

Folks, let me make this clear: The First Amendment is a bitch. Truly. It respects insane, crazy, mean, hateful speech and ideas. Ideas!

The late Johnnie Cochran and I used to spar over this idea. The normally affable Cochran was visibly enraged when I proposed the idea of hate crimes being unconstitutional. I could certainly understand that Johnnie's frame of reference was different from mine, that his life experience would cause him to look rather unkindly at racist venom. Tough. Speech and ideas and thoughts and hate and disdain are all protected by the First Amendment. It's perfectly legal to be an asshole; just don't act on it.

But what degree of animus is relevant to the commission and prosecution of a crime? That indeed is the question. Couldn't any crime be considered a hate crime, because the victim of the crime was targeted specifically?

Say I were to rob an old lady because I hate old ladies. They're old and they're wrinkly and they smell like talcum powder. I hate talcum powder, so I rob her. That's a hate crime, right? Now, say I were to rob an old lady because she's not likely to put up much resistance. I don't have anything against old ladies in general or this old lady in particular. I'm just searching for easy pickings and not targeting a specific group. That wasn't a hate crime, right? Just a crime.

And the difference is . . . ?

The First Amendment's a bitch. It is designed to keep the government from censoring virtually all speech. You know the exceptions: yelling "theater" in a crowded fire, etc. (Kidding.) Regimes, politicians, and judges have for years attempted in many ways to whittle away some of the First's safeguards. And I mean people from all political directions and perspectives. The First Amendment protects so many forms of expression and ideas. It's not just art or books or words that it protects but, in my opinion, campaign funding, political activism and—get this—the ability to be an anti-Semite, racist, homophobe, and even a Republican. It protects ideas. All ideas. Thoughts, perceptions, feelings, misgivings. You can *think* anything you want. Have at it. But when that thought is translated into an act whose prohibition is cognizable at law and already proscribed, the act should be prosecuted, the *actus reus*. The motivation, the impetus, the drive, the reason, the hatred and, again, the cause or even presence of an animus is irrelevant.

The First Amendment must remain intact completely and absolutely for those expressions that we all agree are within its purview. It's under attack from every conceivable direction, but the essence of the First's protections must remain inviolate. When violations of such occur in many cases there's nothing really perceptible. Nothing that grabs you and shakes your conscience. Take hate crimes. The violation, in my very humble opinion, is actually slight and is to many microscopic. It has to be parsed, the violation, that is, and magnified and illuminated. And when that's done you can almost hear the collective "ho hum" of a very bored public. Minorities of all stripes can find this troublesome because it's easy to interpret it as a license to hate. Well, it is. Sorry, as I've said. You can't legislate against hate, only its effects.

IM THE WALRUS

Texting, emailing, and IM'ing were meant to bring us to-gether. BlackBerry devices, cell phones, and the Etch A Sketch were all supposed to facilitate communication in a twenty-first-century *reach out and touch* sort of way. But they haven't. They've pulled us apart. In fact, these little gadgets and gewgaws have forced a wedge between us. A synergistic, atavistic, supercalifragilistic wedge.

Marshall McLuhan (a Canadian, I'm contractually obliged to say), who famously said that the medium was the message, would shit if he saw us now. He'd probably shit if he knew he had a Web site . . . especially one that says "Enter the Me-dium" (and I'm not kidding). These devices haven't enhanced our connections as humans, they've replaced them. Walk down any street and hear the vapid conversations of yammering teenagers, watch thumbs wildly texting hieroglyphic messages. Do you think these people would prefer instead meeting with the person being texted?

Probably not.

It's as though the BlackBerry or PDA or cell phone has become the actual object of our communication, if not the object of our affection. The person on the other end is incidental. Mark my words, one day you'll be able to buy a program that randomly creates artificial, anonymous, computer-generated messages that people will respond to. This knows no analogue. Masturbation? Mime? Marriage? It's like writing a letter to no one and mailing it. No, wait. It's like writing a letter to no one and *not* mailing it. No, it's like writing a letter to no one in invisible ink and not mailing it. Wait! It's like that old print ad (and if you're over forty you will remember this): if u cn rd ths msg u cn bcm a secy n gt a gd jb.

The device has become a proxy, a way of saying, while sitting alone at a bar, "No, I'm not lonely, I'm not friendless, see, I have this cell phone. I'm texting. Don't let my being alone fool you, I'm wanted and needed and speak with legions of people . . . who happen to have opted out of actually sitting next to me." Oh, look! I just got another IM!

Pathetic.

The transmission of information in and of itself is noteworthy and important to us. Years ago, not that many, some office worker had a folded, multigenerational Polack joke that he'd pass around. He had to engage someone personally. He could read the reaction to admittedly politically incorrect humor. He also had to dedicate time to actually reproduce the joke, so it had to be good. Or at least he had to think so. Today, with email, I'm sent jokes that barely qualify as such. Photoshopped Hillary Clintons. Foreign beer commercials. You name it.

To make matters worse, the jokes are not even given to me personally. More often than not I'm included in a mass emailing that's impersonal, unnecessary, unfunny, and shows absolutely no interest in me. What's the difference between a mass email that broadcasts a joke and a mass email that informs me of a belt sander sale at Home Depot? The shipping charges. Again, data for the sake of data is not interpersonal, it's impersonal. It's dissociative and disconnected (not to mention expensive). I'm far from the Luddite and absolutely love new technology. I am rarely without my BlackBerry and always am cell phone–accessible. But I'd rather speak with you personally than IM or text you. Confabulation the old-fashioned way. It's not that I'm an AARP card–totin' old fart (well, yeah, I guess that is true) but that I'm someone who believes in the joy of interpersonal communication.

U 2?

VICE SQUAD

The land of the free and the home of the brave.

Right.

Why is it that the government has such power over our personal habits? Why have we given the legislature so much power over our lives? Doesn't it make you quiver (and not in a good way) that the government tells us that we can't smoke a joint, bet on college hoops, or schedule a trollop for a 3:00 a.m. booty call? I mean, what is more American than that? And yet we just accept it like nodding, obeisant lemmings. We've been brought up for so long with so many personal freedoms being curtailed, limited, and in some cases prohibited altogether; what's a little regulation here and there? After all they're vices. You know . . . faults, depravities, shortcomings, sins, offenses, failings. The stuff Republicans swear they're against. Vice is the opposite of virtue. OK, I get that. But the government doesn't reward us for our virtues, so why should it punish us for our vices?

Let's start with gambling. Football pools, penny-ante poker, roulette, slot machines. Gambling between two or more people is verboten. For the most part. Now, remember there are exceptions to this rule jurisdictionally. But ask: Why is gambling forbidden? Dunno. Not day-trading, mind you. Not speculation, whatever the hell that means. You can "invest" in futures and be back-slapped. But what is gambling other than betting on the future? Of a card. A number. A stock. The hypocrisy makes me sick. Just what is gambling, the gambling that polite society eschews? I'll bet you can't answer that one. We are awash in odds. That's gambling. When Mr. roly-poly weatherman says there's a 20 percent chance of rain . . . hello?

Gambling seems to be no good if available at your house. But have it run by a fictional Indian tribe and *voila*! It's legal, sanctioned, and, oh yeah, helps education. Don't ask me to explain this. Gambling is gambling. Who cares if it's gambling off a scratch card or in the basement of a Catholic church? I have no fucking idea what puritan America has against *some* sorts of gambling. Sorry. I'm still trying to figure out sushi.

I'm a trained lawyer, licensed even, and I'll be damned if I can tell you what exactly the gambling laws are and why they are. Lawyers don't concern themselves with the "why." Why is one form of gambling all right, another not so all right? Just think of it. Dogs, horses, trotters, jai alai, pari-mutuel gaming are fine. And I'll be goddammed if I can parse the exception that pari-mutuel betting enjoys.

Blackjack, poker, roulette, slots: that's fine if it's at a casino or cruise ship that goes so many miles offshore. (Can you believe these rules?!) Lotto, Mega Millions, Take Five, Pick Six, Scratch and Sniff: these are fine also. But gambling is illegal if run by a guy named Vinnie. In big and not-so-big cities around the country there's gambling through bookies and numbers schemes. And they're verboten. Perhaps because the government gets no cut. Fine, then legalize and tax it. State-sanctioned lotteries are fine; the Brooklyn number isn't. Sister Mary Agony at Most Holy Misdemeanor can have bingo every week, but that's different. Why? Beats the fuck out of me.

We've created a monster. We've allowed and, in some cases, insisted that the government control stuff. Our stuff. From Carry Nation and the anti-tipplers to those hunchbacked termagants from wacky chick groups who have a thing about *Girls Gone Wild* videos, there's always been someone screaming, "Hey! Officer! Stop him! He's having fun!" That seems to be the overriding concern: people having fun.

It's critical to a free and thinking society to grasp the fundamental notion that freedom of expression covers more than a racy novel or a burning flag. Expression knows no bounds, so long as children and barn animals are exempt. Consensual expression among adults is limitless in an ideal world.

Now, as to prostitution, this prohibition when deconstructed should amaze and anger you to no end. Let's get our definitions straight. Prostitution is basically sex for compensation or remuneration. Sounds simple enough, right?

Not on your life.

A kept woman or lass who doles out the scootch for support is a mistress. That implies a multiplicity element. If sexual wares are plied exclusively to one john—one at a time—the lady is a prostitute. In house, mistress; street corner, hooker. Or wife, depending upon where you're from. So, the elements are sexual intercourse plus consideration, using the contract law term of art. It's easy to see the blatant and obvious example of prostitution: street hooker says five dollars for a hummer. Tada! Prostitution. Solicitation on the part of the john perhaps. An offer to commit on the part of skank lady.

What about escort services? (And what's wrong with being "escorted"?) They're all over the place and fill the pages of every phone book in the country. How do they get away with it? The cops are too busy (thank God) with other stuff. Massage parlors, what about them? You betcha. Who doesn't know that a "happy ending" is not the conclusion of a Chinese meal? In New York, prostitution is omnipresent. Brothels, escort services, call/outs, it's mind-boggling and allegedly illegal. It's everywhere, yet we pretend that we're doing something about it, that laws are in effect and that society is somehow protected from this nefarious activity.

Now, what about dating? Can't that be construed as prostitution? Absolutely. It depends upon the mind-set and intentions of the participants. What makes streetwalking prostitution so obvious is that the contractual arrangement is made up front. I'll give you $100 for a Cincinnati bowtie. Plain, clear, and simple. But when the payoff or consideration is prospective and not so clear, e.g., dinner and theater for some hoochie-coochie later . . . Hmmm? It's never said that openly and plainly, but the implications can certainly be evident and if such is the case, that's prostitution.

Here's where it gets really interesting. Prostitution is sex for remuneration. Sex. What's sex? No, seriously, what's *sex*? In most states a woman who's paid to role-play is not considered a prostitute. Pay a woman to come over, have her wear jodhpurs and crack a riding crop, all the while singing "Marching to Pretoria" in a Viennese accent. Even if it gets you off spiritually and actually, that's not sex and that's not prostitution. Amazing.

A dominatrix can have a veritable torture chamber in her apartment: wheels affixed to the walls, whips, chains, Great Danes (thanks Martin Mull). So long as there is no "sex," it's not prostitution. No matter how sexually pleasing it was to the patron, this was not sex. Amazing. So the legislators who come up with these laws don't even make the connection that sexual excitement comes in all forms (bad pun). Nope, just don't involve *our* definition of sex and the rest is just fine.

But the issue remains, why can't I as an adult contract with another adult for consensual sex? And what constitutes remuneration or consideration? I know that there are Hollywood types who have been referred to as "arm candy," some chick who's contracted to show up at a premiere on the arm of some guy. You know that sex is certainly an aspect of this. After the event he knocks the bottom out of chickie. Isn't this prostitution? I sure think it is. The consideration was her exposure in magazines and the like. Walk with me down the aisle, pretend to be my lady friend, I'll schtupp you later and you get recognition and exposure. That's your consideration. That's your remuneration. That's prostitution.

But stop.

Don't miss the point.

How have we gotten this far? How have we abnegated the fundamental and natural right to contract with each other whether it's for sex or friendship or what have you? How basic is it to be able to negotiate with an adult over the panoply of services, relationships, and things? Here's a fiver; be Eleanor Roosevelt (again). Here's a large, pretend you're a French maid who's been caught by an Alsatian group and is forced to speak Esperanto upside down while wearing a merkin. So long as it's not involving "sex" it's OK. Sex. You know, *sex*. How have we let the government intervene under its police power authority to prohibit interpersonal relationships that, yes, are even paid for? This isn't about personal feelings towards prostitution or gambling or gay marriage even or the ability to wear white after Labor Day. It's about relinquishing freedom to a government that we have been duped into trusting. As a matter of personal disclosure, I find the idea of prostitution most distasteful. But that's for me to decide. I find it pathetic that I'd have to go and pay a woman to pretend that she finds me attractive. Maybe I'm old-fashioned, but part of the pleasure of adult sex is the idea that a woman would want to have sex with me without a monetary incentive. But that's for me to decide. I have never had a lap dance and don't particularly care for gentlemen's clubs. I find them dreary and their denizens pathetic. But, again, that's my preference and up to me to decide. It's not for a government to review for their consideration.

There is nothing that defines my philosophy better than this: So long as you don't hurt anyone, do whatever you want. I may not get it or agree with it or do it, just don't hurt anyone. Don't hurt a kid, an animal, or me.

And let the government tax it.

CLOSE ENCOUNTERS
OF THE ABSURD KIND

UFO's. How did UFO—which means, as we all know, Unidentified Flying Object—come to mean simply and only spaceships? We're talking about aliens in spaceships. ET's, Martians, spacemen. Little green men with antennae. Ray Walston. My Favorite Martian. Danger, Will Robinson! You get it.

But wait a minute.

I'm just an innocent bystander in all this and not a trained professional, but it seems to me that there must be some unidentified flying objects that, once identified, don't turn out to be vehicles from other planets. What about everyone's favorite: the ubiquitous weather balloon? It seems that that's the answer for everything. Just how many of these buggers have been deployed? The Air Force's Project Blue Book—it should have been called Project Bullshit—attributes virtually everything to weather balloons. Thousands upon thousands of aircraft with amazing light systems speed through the skies at incredible speeds and they are all weather balloons. So, while I think that many of the unidentified are certainly identifiable, I must say that I am a tad skeptical when I hear the "official" reason cited. Kinda like 9/11. But that's for another book. Let me also throw this thought out: Just because an object that flies is identified, doesn't mean it's *not* an alien craft.

Don't get me wrong. I want there to be actual communicative aliens who can land and interact with us and explain how we can cure cancer, save the planet from destruction, and maybe, just maybe, explain the phenomenon of sushi. I'm a tad conflicted. How can so many people, rational people like Jimmy Carter (OK, bad example), say they've seen something that was, er, unusual? Believe me, the idea that there are other life-forms, and I'm not talking bacteria here, in the vast universe is certainly plausible. I know you've seen the Drake Equation and if you haven't LOOK IT UP! It states that the probability of there being alternative life-forms is at least mathematically possible when you include all the various factors (number of stars, planets, galaxies, etc.). But there also exists a concomitant hypothesis, yes, possible indeed, that we are the only life-form in the universe. Let's continue.

The question must be asked: Has there ever been a spacecraft driven by some Martian type that landed here? No. Repeat, nope. Never happened. At least, it has never been documented. Really documented, not merely hearsay or anecdotal. None other than Carl Sagan said that extraordinary claims require extraordinary evidence. I mean, don't you think that some relic of the tens of thousands of reported (emphasis on *reported*) sightings would have revealed some, oh, I don't know, EVIDENCE? Tangled wreckage (these things never crash), maybe. A captured alien. Anything. Oh, yeah, what about Area 51?

As everyone with a pulse knows, Area 51 is contained within the Air Force's Nevada test and training range. It's where evidence of alien stuff including the crashed craft from Roswell, New Mexico, allegedly is stored. Look, this isn't a book on UFO's so research elsewhere if this interests you. The point is that all we know is the names of these places that purportedly are the sites of alien visits or house remnants of their craft. Again, evidence? None. The government swears there's nothing and has refused to make any evidence available. And don't even think of suggesting that the government should come clean with its information. Just ask Dennis Kucinich, who suggested that very thing during his failed bid to be the 2008 Democratic presidential nominee. They laughed him off the stage and out of the race. (I know, there were other reasons for it too.)

But is it possible? Possible that there are alien beings who are out there and have been here? Sure. Does the government routinely lie to us and hide information? Uh-huh. But that's all we know. In a court of law, there could be no verdict on the existence of aliens with what we "know." It's all what we think, what we think is hidden, and what people say they saw. And, oh yeah, don't forget the grainy video. That's the totality of evidence.

When the reports of these "aliens" are reviewed a number of striking similarities come to light—similarities, in fact, that negate any chance of the stories being real. You see, as a prosecutor I noticed a few things when people report something that occurred. Say, an armed robbery. Individuals repeat their own stories almost verbatim with little, if any, variation. But the stories of those who all witnessed the same event vary. Sometimes greatly. What is so amazing about the various alien accounts is that they seem to have been rehearsed, reiterated, and regurgitated. The same story. Over and over again. And, remember, I want there to be aliens, I mean it, but it's all anecdotal, identically anecdotal, and there's no FUCKING EVIDENCE!

For starters, aliens are fascinated by our anuses. That's what I've heard from witness "accounts." These little guys fly millions (billions?) of miles across time and space, only to abduct unfortunate earthlings and head straight for . . . our backsides?! Seems implausible, doesn't it? Yet according to all

accounts these interstellar critters invariably involve themselves in anal probing. Every time I hear of these cloacal
explorations I laugh hysterically. Hysterically, I tell you. Honestly, this cracks me up. It's a bum rap. (Okay, those were
pretty cheap puns, *butt* what the hell.)

These are some pretty sharp cookies that've mastered flying through the universe at near-speed-of-light velocities and
once here find bunghole mapping priority number one. Go
figure.

And can I ask you this? Why does ET have no interest in
ever landing? Why does he just want to fly around and terrorize? All that travel, all that time spent cramped into a
spaceship and you think he'd want to get out and stretch his
legs.

And why no interest in speaking with leaders of countries
or dignitaries? They care not for scientists or fellow space
travelers. Don't you think they'd like to hop over to NASA
and laugh their asses off at our interstellar jalopies? We hear
they come in peace. At least that's what all the old sci-fi black
and whites promised us. So why not extend a grey paw in
friendship? Land, dammit! Nope. Instead they want to yuck
it up with some agrestic trailer-bat named Jethro in the middle of nowhere and scare the shit out of Ma Kettle. Strange
for incredibly smart people, don't you think?

And another thing. Seems that these beings have configured their craft in such a way that it is incapable of being

photographed with any degree of clarity. Stealth technology at its finest, maybe? No camcorder operator or photographer can capture any footage or still image that presents anything cognizable as anything to anyone. No digital camera. No cell phone camera. The photo libraries of Earth are replete with blurred lights and amazing hubcap-shaped images. Makes you think, doesn't it? Every time some Hollywood D-lister climbs out of a car *sans* panties and exposes her scootch, we've at least a hundred photos. When some over-stressed mom whales on her kid in a Wal-Mart parking lot, we've loads of security cameras. Our entire world is under continuous surveillance and not one alien picture worth a damn. Not one. (Funny, there's no really good video or photo of a plane hitting the Pentagon on 9/11 either. For a later book.)

If you really want to believe in these space creatures, take out your calculator and do the math. The distances that would have to be traversed for them to reach us are mind-boggling. Even if traveling at or very near the speed of light. That's 186,000 miles per *second*. Maybe these space fellers knew how to slip through wormholes and black holes, somehow finding interstellar shortcuts (which is absurd, but let's assume *arguendo*). Don't even compare it to our air and space travel. (Imagine the number of on-time departures. And the security checks!) I'll just assume these space guys can do anything. And then just imagine the deceleration of a space vehicle from those speeds. OK, let's say they traveled at one-tenth the speed of light, it's still inconceivable. These ships seem to stop on a dime. From one-tenth the speed of light, no less. And the energy that a spaceship would have to have on board, keeping in mind that midflight refueling is a tad far-fetched (as is this entire fantasy), is beyond funny. And, I harp on it, admittedly, after all this travel they DON'T LAND!

But, I'm not being fair. They do land on farms and in really, really rural patches. And, oh yeah, they've no GPS and need crop circles to identify which hillbilly family to terrorize. They can find their way here, but need additional information as to Jed Clampett's address.

But how many of us say that we "believe" in UFO's? Believe in what? There's just gotta be, right?

The next thing you'll tell me is that you believe in God.

If atheism is a religion, then not collecting stamps is a hobby.

—Unknown

GOOD NEWS! A DUI STORY

DUI is driving under the influence. An IUD is an intra-uterine device. That's all you need to know to appreciate this phone call I received from a friend of mine. All true.

> FRIEND: "Good news! My girlfriend ___ got a DUI."
>
> ME: "That's terrible."
>
> FRIEND: "Terrible?! Why?"
>
> ME: "Do you know what that means?"
>
> FRIEND: "Oh, *I* know what that means."
>
> ME: "Her insurance rates are going to go up."
>
> FRIEND: "What?! Why?"
>
> ME: "Because she's a bigger risk."
>
> FRIEND: "A risk of what?"
>
> ME: "Look, can I help you?"

FRIEND: "Help me?! With what?!"

ME: "Look, where did it happen?"

FRIEND: "At the doctor's office."

ME: "You mean in front?"[1]

FRIEND: "No inside."

ME: "He followed you *inside*?!"[2]

FRIEND: "No, he was already inside."[3]

ME: "What the hell are you talking about?"

FRIEND: "That contraceptive thing that's inserted into a woman."

ME: "You mean an IUD."

FRIEND: "That's what I said."

ME: "No, you said DUI."

Hysterical laughter ensued. Choking, gasping chortling. Cachinnations. Guffaws. You name it. We couldn't breathe. He made one request.

FRIEND: "Promise you'll never tell anyone."

ME: "Sure. I promise."

---

[1] This was critical because case law at the time was undecided if a DUI could be charged on private property as opposed to a public road or thoroughfare.

[2] *Ibid.*

[3] Entrapment? Was this an inside job? Why was she drunk at her doctor's office?

A PUBLIC APOLOGY TO MY SISTER

On August 26, 1970, my twelfth birthday, I was preparing for my party. Relatives, mainly, were to arrive in the immediate future. My chore was to vacuum our "Florida room." People from "Flawda" will recognize this term immediately.

My sister, then ten, had tried for years to grow her hair long. She was obsessed over the length of her hair. She adored Cher's locks and wanted more than anything else to have long hair like hers. She fanaticized about it well into her forties. (Sorry, Sis, that was a joke.) But she truly wanted long hair. Long-flowing, over the shoulder, Buffy Sainte-Marie, Cher hair. Bless her heart, she wore towels she imagined as her natural hair. Wigs. Branches and twigs even. All right I'm kidding about the last part. But it seems she finally made "headway" and her hair was finally shoulder-length. She was so proud.

My sister was looking for a phone book that was under a couch. Seems I was vacuuming the carpet directly in front of her. She was looking under the couch and her then almost-long hair lay on the carpet directly in front of my upright Hoover. For reasons that to this day are unknown to me, reasons that I can't for the life of me fathom, I saw her hair and the Hoover and thought, well, hair-Hoover, hair-Hoover. Hmmm?

Guess what I did?

Yep.

Before I go into details, let me first address the configuration of the vacuum cleaner. This was an old-fashioned nuclear-powered super-Hoover with beaters. It possessed the suction of a small turbine jet engine. It knows no peer today. It was a seventies upright. "Don't spare the horsepower" was the battle cry. Oreck schmoreck! This baby could kill.

Look. You have to understand the zeitgeist. The seventies were nothing like the hypervigilant times we live in now, when parents insist their children wear a bike helmet while making a peanut butter sandwich. Correction—when parents insist their children wear a bike helmet while the nanny makes a peanut butter sandwich. This was the seventies, and not only could I use the Hoover without a license or adult supervision, I could pass the Hoover over my sister's hair. It was a rough and tumble time when parents thought nothing of giving high-powered weapons to their kids.

Meanwhile back at the ranch.

As the first of my sister's hair became entangled and twisted and enwrapped in the beaters, it naturally jammed. The motor froze as did the expression on my sister's face. Frozen in a hideous silent howl. Think Al Pacino in the last scene of the dreadful *Godfather III*. Or Edvard Munch's "The Scream." Or you when you get your first credit card bill after the holidays. Frozen, I tell you. The time that elapsed between the initial entanglement of hair and her first utterance of a shriek followed by bone-chilling screams seemed a lifetime. Time stopped.

It was a sensory-overload moment. Audiovisual stimuli (her shrieking) followed olfactory. You know the smell that an electric motor makes when it burns out or is jammed, that of something burning, a metallic singeing? Yeah, well it was that in spades.

Now let's think about the scene my mother walked into upon hearing my sister's tortured anguish. My sister was prone on the floor, her hair was inextricably enlaced in the beaters of the upright, the smell of fried electric motor wafted therefrom. Screaming, howling. And all the while, I stood there with a look that must have said, "I know this looks bad, but I have a perfectly logical explanation for why it appears I've scalped my sister."

My mother was never a violent person and never hit or spanked me in anger. She's a kind woman at heart and has shown incredible patience with me throughout my life. But the look she gave me that afternoon was bloodcurdlingly terrifying. To her credit (and my amazement), she didn't lay a hand on me. But if looks could kill, this would be written posthumously.

The task at hand was obvious: to extricate my sister's head from the Hoover upright. My mother first suggested cutting my sister's hair from the beater blades. What?! The hair that took my sister years to grow? Her now shoulder-length locks sheared?! Not on your life, my sister begged. So with the deft touch of a surgeon my mother knelt down and she and I began the dethreading process, carefully pulling short lengths from the blades without the use of scissors. This was a painstaking process. Like making a ship in a bottle or reattaching a limb. It was amazing how far up the Hoover's system my sister's hair was entangled. Meanwhile, minutes ticked away what seemed at an accelerated rate. My birthday guests would be arriving shortly.

My mother would pull out a length of hair and give me the death glare. All the while my sister was contorted in a most uncomfortable position that permitted by mother to unthread her hair with the base of the monster vac inches from her head. If this were the current decade they would have made a reality TV show about it. Finally, my sister was rescued from the bear trap of the Hoover, her hair intact. Though I must say she sported a rather unique wave thereafter. I'm relieved to note that my sister suffered no permanent brain damage after the incident, although after the event she spoke with an Alsatian accent, walked with a noticeable limp, and didn't blink for a year. With my sister dazed and relieved over her escape, my mother ordered me outside—"Out of my sight!" was what she actually said—while the final preparations for my party were made. I sat outside in the August heat sobbing in a state of shock and terror.

Would my mother snap?

What fate awaited upon my return?

What to do?

There was always the witness protection program or joining an Amish community.

When my guests arrived I was huddled outside our kitchen door, crying. Their looks of celebratory happiness and congratulations were immediately erased after my mother opened the door and shouted, "Don't talk to him!" Do not talk to the birthday boy. Do not speak to the man of the hour. Say nothing to he whose life you celebrate. After a while I returned to the "festivities," all the while avoiding eye contact with my furious mother. My cake was placed, rather, slammed, I must say, on the kitchen table, the candles lighted, and my mother commenced a rendition of "Happy Birthday" that had the tenderness of, oh, Marilyn Manson.

I'll never forget that day, and neither will my sister.

I'm sorry, Sis.

I COULDN'T CARE LESS

I could care less.

It drives me nuts. You've heard it a million times and may even have used this nonsensical phrase. And what's even scarier is that it's becoming not only more commonplace than the original expression (you know, the one that actually makes sense), but accepted as a valid alternative. And it makes absolutely no sense. None. I don't have to remind you that if you could care less, what's the big deal? Why even mention it?

Let's all repeat: I ***couldn't*** care less.

Say it a hundred times if you have to. Let's all take an oath and pledge to rid our world of this idiotic phrase once and for all.

While we're at it: Please, I beg you. Lose *irregardless*. I'm not going to bore you with its own illogical construction, the double negative. I won't. I know, I know. It's a weird conflation of *irrespective* and *regardless*, but something tells me that anyone stupid enough to say *irregardless* never heard of *irrespective*. Former Arkansas governor Mike Huckabee repeated "irregardless" at least thrice in a sentence once and no one batted an eye. Forget the fact that this affable rube wanted to be President of the U. S. of A. Forget the fact that if he's too stupid to not know how stupid "irregardless" is, what other critical facts must he not know? No, not one mention was made. But had the Huckster dropped a well-placed and precisely used F-bomb, we would never have heard the end of it.

It's gotten so bad that most dictionaries recognize *irregardless* as "informal." Informal?! Look what's happening to us. Instead of remaining steadfast in demanding correct usage, we give in. Concede. Throw in the towel. Jesus! Look how we've become slackers. *Irregarding* the loss of our language, it gets worse.

Look, a neologism is one thing and perfectly fine: That's a new word or phrase. *Phone tag. Blogosphere. Cincinnati bowtie. Reach around. Bukkake.* But there are alternative pronunciations of words and expressions that don't exist or make the slightest sense. And what happens when a word or expression is used with almost universal frequency? It's accepted as an alternative.

Bullshit.

It's even happened with *zoology*. Dictionaries have included *zoo-ology* as a variation. No, *zoo-ology* requires just that: three *o*'s. Thank God these cretins haven't heard of the oophorectomy or it would likewise fall victim to the *oo-*phorectomy.

Accusations always follow attempts at correcting our idiocy. You're being priggish. Pedantic. Nitpicky. Pathologically punctilious. It seems nobody gives a shit about our mother tongue. After Dubya killed me with "nucular"—of or pertaining to a *nucule* (?!)—and people thought it quaint that he was so simple and down to earth (more "simpleton," if you ask me), it's high time for us to reclaim what is ours.

Our language.

I *couldn't* care less if you use profanity so long as it's correctly used. After all, a well-placed *fuck* (I know, I know) can be beautiful . . . if used correctly.

Maybe it's me, but I hear a lot of *supposably* lately. Not *supposedly*, but *supposably*. Able to be supposed? Look, we all have our "favorites." I have a friend who goes ballistic when she hears "world-wind" versus "whirlwind." A judge friend showed me a memo that his legal secretary wrote that said he would not "continence" that ruling. (And speaking of legal secretaries, one woman I know typed a letter for her boss that, I kid you not, ended with "I will keep you abreast of the situation orally." Talk about support staff . . . yuk . . .) I actually read in a newspaper that New York mayor Rudy (9/11)

Giuliani had "prostrate" surgery. Funny, I thought he'd be supine. Either way, it sure beats the hell out of standing.

I cringe at "aks" versus "ask." Some have suggested that it's a racist thing if I find fault with this mispronunciation and misusage because it's often associated with urban speech. That's bullshit. Why? Because it's wrong, no matter who says it. Plain and simple. Imagine JFK in his great speech imploring us to *aks* not what our country can do for us. No, *aks* is not a word and it's not a mispronunciation. (There's a Lizzie Borden joke here somewhere.) Another thing: *heighth* simply does not exist. *Length* and *width* fine.

And while we're at it:

It's	Not
pollute	plute
a blessing in disguise	a blessing in the skies
across	acrossed
barbed wire	bob wire
affidavit	afterdavid
candidate	cannidate
espresso	Xpresso
jibe	jive
law and order	Laura Norder
drown	drownd
escape	excape
supposedly	supposably

It's	Not
interpret	interpretate
Heimlich maneuver	Henniken maneuver
film	fillum
miniature	minature
for all intents and purposes	for all intensive purposes

A mispronunciation is one thing. *Tomato, potato, often, Louisville, Missouri* even (though I don't get the Missoura thing). As far as Louisville, how is the capital of Kentucky pronounced? (Pause) Frankfort. (Rim shot)

I understand that *Wednesday* isn't pronounced as such nor is *February*. And I've never gotten a handle on *catsup* and *ketchup* and don't know anyone who ever asked for a *bologna* sandwich. *Sangwich* in some parts.

I have New York friends who swear I hail from *Tampar*, Florida. JFK was most concerned with Castro's *Cuber*.

Look, let's not miss the point here. The point is that we in our country *couldn't* care less about what is actual, preferred, and correct. Our language and its rules are trifling to many. Big deal. After all, when Bush 43 went *nucular*, this cacoepy was unimportant. We hear of the dreaded French who take great umbrage at stupid Americans who butcher their language. Well, good for them. There's nothing silly about demanding that people know and speak our language, even if we are those people. No one's talking about such linguistic peccadilloes as ending a sentence with a preposition. What I'm suggesting is that we all commit ourselves to paying attention to what we're saying and how we're saying it irregardless of who we are and where we're from.

LIONEL LAW: Texting "How R U?" does not constitute contact, any more than ramen noodles constitute a nutritious meal.

THE FIRST AMENDMENT'S A BITCH

Son of Sam. Damn him. Not only for the rash of senseless killings that paralyzed New York City in the late 1970s, but for being responsible for one of the most unbelievably unconstitutional laws in existence. Son of Sam Laws violate the very spirit of the First Amendment. They penalize free speech. Yeah, even a homicidal maniac's free speech. Not that it was your idea, Berkowitz, but damn you anyway.

(By the way, never, ever have anything named after you. A law, disease, nothing. The latter goes without saying. It's never good. Just ask Lou Gehrig.)

Now let's get back to Son of Sam Laws. Here's the story. Americans believe that a criminal should not be able to profit from his crime in any way. From the immediate proceeds of the offense (say, theft or drug sales), to selling the story to

Hollywood, to pitching a book, or even selling prison art-work, criminals should not benefit from their miscreant ways. Period. This theory centers around monetary benefit(s). After all, if some lunatic kills a family and writes a book about it, all proceeds from the sale of that story should go to the surviving family members (or the state) and not to the person who perpetrated the crime. After all, it would be blood money, right? Sounds logical. Until, of course, you think about it.

No one should benefit financially from his crime. No one should be able to write a book or screenplay about the crime he was convicted of. Right?

Hmmm? Let's see, who would fall under this category?

+ **Jesus**
+ **Saint Paul**
+ **Mahatma Gandhi**
+ **Rosa Parks**
+ **Martin Luther King, Jr.**
+ **Adolph Hitler**

Quite a list, eh? And they're all convicted criminals.

Wait, I hear you scream. You can't possibly compare Hit-ler with St. Paul. And Jesus? Jesus in the same category with Hitler?! You can't do that! You can't put them in the same category with Hitler for Chrissakes! (Sorry.)

Can. And did.

Look, each of these folks was charged with and convicted of a crime. They then wrote about those crimes. Each one. Read the list again. Son of Sam Laws would have prevented each one from enjoying the monetary profits of their works. Monetary profits that could be used to help spring them, the innocent. Son of Sam Laws focus in on the convicted and the incarcerated. No matter who they are or what they were convicted of.

The fact remains, Cochise, that all speech, repeat, ALL speech must remain unfettered, unencumbered and, oh yes, that title again, free. No one ever loses the right to speech. No one. No matter who you are or what you did, from Albert Fish to Cindy Sheehan to Regis Philbin, your arrest and conviction for anything—*anything*—shall in no wise stifle, prevent, proscribe, or limit your speech.

Wait! (I can just hear you now.) What if we just limited the dirtbag's ability to make money from the speech? Sure, let him speak all he wants, but he never sees a dime of the payoff. And after all, what good is a $50,000 book advance to Charles Manson? How much money can his prison canteen fund hold? Why should said dirtbag benefit monetarily? You mean that dirtbag Jesus? Of course not, you insist. Oh—you mean that villainous lawbreaker Dr. Martin Luther King, Jr.? Or Rosa Parks? Now, she scares me. Oh . . . I get it. You mean the real nasty, nefarious guilty dirtbag who's arrested and convicted of a crime we can all agree now is, well, crimeworthy. (Whatever the hell that means.)

It sounds so simple—all proceeds of any and all sales of said "speech" go directly to victim families or into a trust for _____ (fill in the blank).

It sounds so simple, but it's not.

First, let's come up with a few gray areas, shall we?

Suppose some miscreant writes a book declaring his innocence. Suppose it's a best seller. Suppose all proceeds were to go to his criminal appeal. Suppose he's actually innocent. That book and its proceeds got him sprung. Why should he have to forfeit profits that proved him innocent? Because remember, he was convicted at first.

Suppose further a felon was convicted of a crime we like, e.g., trespassing on an animal-experimentation facility (hello, PETA), or refusing to pay taxes under the belief that his taxes were supporting something unconstitutional. I'm not crazy about any of these hypotheticals, but some people feel that those behaviors are commendable and laudable. Under Son of Sam Laws, too bad. No remunerated speech.

We're done supposing.

Now *assume* a vile, multiply convicted child predator waives all fees from the sale of a screenplay or book. He doesn't want "payment," he wants recognition. Keep the money, he says, just let me bask in the glory of being America's new public enemy number one. (Wait, isn't that a Fox reality show?) What do we do with this character? He's profiting from fame. Can we secure a lien on fame? Or do we merely tell the jerk to shut up? His payment, his remuneration is in notoriety. What do we do then?

Another convicted felon, a heinous one at that, wants to write a tell-all book warning kids to not do what he's done. Commendable? Maybe. But that doesn't answer the question: What happens to the proceeds?

So what do we do, then, Einstein? Or better yet, Mr. Constitutional pansy, what would *you* suggest?

Thanks for asking. OK, here goes. Ready? Here comes the answer.

Sue the bastard.

Yup, sue him; get a judgment that acts as a lien in most jurisdictions for twenty years or more, and anything he receives thereafter—book proceeds, Lotto payouts, inheritance—goes right to the judgment holder, the victim or his family. Tada! If someone victimized you, sue the bastard.

We're not finished yet.

If we take Son of Sam Laws to their extreme, why should *anyone* profit from a criminal act? Why should anyone collect on the misdeeds of others? Why should there be derivative beneficiaries who traffic in the vile behavior of others too dumb to get away with it? We haven't gotten there yet. Let us pray.

But think about it. The New York Public Library has, I'm

sure, at least one copy of *Mein Kampf.* Are they "profiting"? You bet. As do we when we can refer to the very words of a mad man. Lest we forget.

When Dr. King wrote "Letter from Birmingham Jail," let's face it, he was a criminal. Convicted at that. Yes, under stupid laws at the time no doubt, but a convicted criminal he was nonetheless. But how do we parse the issues of which crime and historical context would apply to Son of Sam Laws? Do we like the person? Is he a latter-day hero? What this is all about is stopping some bastard from profiting in any way from his awful crime. But my bastard may be your hero. Who decides?

Moreover, the issue remains whether capturing profits from someone who "benefits" from their crime is contrary to the First Amendment. Is it unconstitutional to let a convicted felon speak but seize all profits from such?

You betcha.

When you squelch profit, you discourage speech. And speech is a bitch, make no mistake. When the government says that one person cannot enjoy the usual rewards of speech, in this case profits, it's limiting speech. I know this will drive many crazy, but don't worry. It's not a very long ride.

Conduct should have consequences, monetary and otherwise. Protected speech shouldn't. It should be unencumbered, limitless, and unfettered by the government swooping in as public pirates.

Remember, sue the bastards. Then their conduct will have consequences. Civil liability punishes conduct by attaching wages, profits, and assets. More importantly, the plaintiffs are the victim and his family. Not the government. The family sues and recovers through monetary damages for the wrong the criminal has committed against them. Not the government. The family captures all the criminal's assets, speech-related or not. Not the government.

The First Amendment, the glorious First Amendment, knows not the benefactor of its protection. Not the rapscallion, the demon, the poet, nor the sage. It protects all and their speech.

The First Amendment's a bitch.

URETHRA FRANKLIN: NO R.E.S.P.E.C.T.

When I was thirteen I had a physical, peed into a cup, and my doctor noticed I had white blood cells in my urine. I thought, well, good. Cells. White at that. Good. Wrong. All was not good. At all. Seems that white blood cells indicated infection, plague, death, or something not the least preferred. My doctor wanted to take a *picture* of my bladder. To see if all was OK. You know, an X-ray. Big deal, right?

X-rays. So what. Hold your breath. Turn your head and cough. Big deal. Well, welcome to the voiding cystogram. This procedure makes waterboarding look like listening to Vikki Carr. Here's how it works.

A catheter, or a Foley as it's called, is a twelve-mile-long tube that's threaded through your pizzle, through the meatus (the hole), then the urethra (the tube). All six miles of urethra. It's threaded through your Jimmy until it hits the bladder. It's a serpentine tube that's lubed and shoved up your WMD, plain and simple. As you sit there, rather, lie there, legs spread, dignity but a memory, a technician wearing gloves slathers a lube over the end of this hose, grabs your knob, and sends it south. Or is it north? You can't believe the pain. No anesthesia, no topical anything, nada. Just cold plastic violating Mr. Happy.

Finally, they hit pay dirt. The bladder. Ah, a welcome respite, right? Not so fast, Tonto. The schvantz-end of said tube is then affixed to a bag, at that time (think the seventies) a bottle, of contrast. Contrast: that's radiology-speak for a goop that shows up on the X-ray that documents this medieval sexual violation. Your bladder is then filled with said goop and it takes forever.

Now, a note on bladder tension. Imagine the worst pee you ever had to take. A long bus trip or waiting for your editrix to get back to you with chapter edits. Remember how you thought you would burst? Remember that incredible, inexplicable pressure? Well, that ain't nothing compared to having your bladder actually filled and distended with radioactive gel. Every, no, really, *every* square inch of said bladder is filled. Every centimeter, every crevice, every fold. Every interstitial you name it is filled. To capacity. And I mean capacity. And the pain? Agony describes the pain like stupid does Dubya. It doesn't even come close.

Now when all this was happening the tech left the room and told me that if I were to become "uncomfortable" to just let her know. As you might have guessed, I informed this person that I was and had been uncomfortable from the get-go. Seems that someone had shoved a garden hose in my barely post-adolescent rooster and *ergo* discomfort thereafter ensued. Haha! She left. And I will never forget the sound of that door closing. That door, that radiology suite door shutting. A thump, a thud. It was the sound of a room being sealed shut. From radiological bleed-through. From . . . sound. The sound of a thirteen-year-old young man screaming in pain whilst a hose violated him all the while filling his bladder with something that would scare the shit out of Madame Curie. I yelled, I panicked. I said I was in pain. I was, after all, uncomfortable.

Then . . . silence. No one came. No one answered my entreaties to return, to unhook and untether me from this ghastly torture. Why? Because by law radiology suites must be so thick as to prevent radiological seepage. They must be bomb-shelter thick. Soundproof. Get it? Oh, shit, I remember thinking. Oh, shit.

After what seemed like the proverbial eternity a Florence Nightingale came back and said, "Oh." That's right, "Oh." Not "Oh, fuck." "Oh, sorry." "Oh, I apologize for the fact that your abdomen has distended to the size of Roseanne." Just "Oh."

And it wasn't pain. It was the feeling of being about to rupture. To give birth. Think *Alien*. Think geyser. Ol' Faithful. Again, Roseanne, if you must. The radiologist came in. Took those "pictures" and then proceeded to slip, no, yank the catheter out from me. And he said the most beautiful words I've ever heard.

He said: You may now "void." See, that's urology-speak for piss. Piss like that racehorse you've spoken of. Piss like Niagara. Piss with a stream whose fury rivals that of ladder companies. It so happens that I performed said piss in a bathroom at St. Joseph's Hospital in Tampa that must have been designed by Phil Spector à la his wall of sound. This cubicle was ceramically tiled and provided a baffled sound booth that visitors to St. Joe's still speak of. I unloaded six gallons—no, I exaggerate—four gallons of urine with a ferocity and intensity that could have permitted me to sand-etch or engrave valuables.

Remember, if your doctor ever says he's found white cells in your urine . . . run.

But wait, I almost forgot. Do you know what they found after this Guantánamo torture session? A diverticulum.

Film at 11.

HIS AND HERS

Men are mutant women. Don't believe me? XX chromosomes produce women. XY's end up as men. The Y chromosome is for the most part genetically inert. It thwarts the completion of an intact woman. We're women until the sixth week of gestation when Mr. Y chromosome interrupts the development of a woman. Yep, men are mutant women with nipples and genital homologues. Sorry, fellas.

It may bother some of you to harp on biological differences. That's just silly. The notion of equality may be true at the legislative level or the polling booth, but we are definitely not equal or alike or even vaguely similar. New biometric studies are showing palpable, identifiable differences between gay and straight men from index finger to ring finger ratios, hair whorling, penchant for show tunes, you name it. And

Playboy magazine has shown real, identifiable differences between men and women. They're different in more ways than you can even count. And we're not talking biological here. We're talking emotionally, psychically, and behaviorally antithetical.

Intrigued?

Let's look at some amazing differences between chicks and dicks.

Women exhibit an absolutely insane fetish over shoes. Sure, this sounds typically misogynistic, but it's true. Yeah, there are those 2 percent of women who defy this truth, but for some reason what women wear on their feet captivates their attention and imagination like nothing we men can ever fathom. Ask a man how many pairs of shoes he has (excluding gym shoes) and I'm betting he'll say two: one black pair and one brown pair. Now, if this were 1976 chances are your respondent would say three, but thank God platform shoes went out with disco, so most self-respecting men will answer *two*. In fact, I'd say 98 percent will say two pair. Ask a man when was the last time he walked by a window display and *had* to have those cordovans.

There are, however, two areas of fascination for all men: barbecues and car engines. If you want to see men join in almost hypnotically, either (a) pull out some charcoal and lighter fluid and start a barbecue or (b) lift the hood of a car in a thinly veiled attempt at automobile maintenance or repair. The former may have some early, caveman reference, perhaps, while the latter is just goofy. Most guys have nary a clue as to how engines work and couldn't distinguish a distributor cap from a manifold (nor can I), but pop that hood and watch the swarm. While we're at it, any earth-moving or construction equipment will hypnotize men. You can see it even in little boys who've never seen a truck but just love them as toys. Girls, well, they're different; they don't get it.

As for colors, women can have the vocabulary of a tree sloth for ordinary, run-of-the-mill words. But when it comes to colors, they have a genius to articulate the most incredible gradations of chromatic variation. Biscuit. Ecru. Buff. Fawn. Camel. Neutral. Caramel. Cinnamon. Coffee. Mushroom. Sand. Men have no clue as to what general groups those colors denote. Most men will have absolutely no idea that these are all words for . . . beige. A friend says that men are Windows 16, named after what he calls the original basic 16 colors that came with original Microsoft Windows programs. We're black, brown, and green. Purple's about as exotic as we get.

Women are suspicious of each other and are predatory. Men are gregarious. It's part of our stupidity. Women are smarter than men and are conspiratorial by nature. They trust none of their sisters and their default programming begins with doubt. Men slap each other on the back at first and may become suspicious later on. Women are hard-wired for nongregarious behavior. It benefits the species for women to be homebodies and not gregarious peregrinators. Women who are able to focus on their brood to the exclusion of others evolutionarily are superior and those traits are preferred.

Women tend to eschew porn. The "men are visual" mantra is absolutely true. So devoid of imagination are men that eroticism must be graphically depicted in medical textbook close-ups and redundant, obvious, up-close-and-personal videography. Women can enjoy a novel. They can imagine. It's the symbolic superstructure of the event that piques their interest, not the "no-shit" truncheoning that so dominates porn. Women tend not to frequent male strip clubs. First, because there are none except for the occasional Chippendales thing (and by the way, they're all gay, he says dismissively) and second because the idea of some guy shaking his schlong in a woman's face is rather not preferred. Penises are weapons and can be viewed as threatening and invasive. Take my word for it.

Women are great talkers. There has never been a man who hasn't at some point wanted to scream "Shut the fuck up!" Yammering, bleating, nonstop yakking; it's inherent in women. And this makes sense. Women must have the ability to communicate with their young. Again, it's atavistic. It's an evolutionary and primordial trait that nature prefers and encourages. They're so good at expressing themselves (a very good trait in raising kids), they can't stop.

Women are obsessed with their breasts, men their penises. No matter how many times women hear that breast size is not important on the whole to most men, they obsess over their boobs nonetheless. Oh, there are some cretins who insist that their wife have a certain cup size. I don't get it. Mammoplasty is akin to artificially inserting synthetic biceps in one's arms. What man would seriously think that that counts or is a valid substitute for the real thing? Men constantly joke about penis size, refer to penis size; they are indeed phallocentric. And no matter how many times women say that penis size doesn't matter (barring the extreme ends of the mentulate spectrum), men disregard it.

Women have no inherent ability to tell jokes. Nor do they know any jokes. There are the exceptions. Let's see, at last check there were three women on the planet who could tell jokes. I have no idea what the disconnect is here. The setup, the delivery, perhaps the imagery that's involved might play roles. Maybe because jokes tend to be slapstick in many respects (translation: cruel). Women loathe the Three Stooges. Think of it; when did you last see your girlfriend, sister, wife, or acquaintance in the throes of hysterical laughter? See? When was the last time you recall a chortle, a cachinnation, even a guffaw? Whatever that primordial connection is that permits men to laugh, really laugh, or to tell or receive jokes, women are without it. Look at stand-up comics. Of the few female stand-ups, I submit that a disproportionate percentage are lesbian. No, this isn't sexist or homophobic. Think about it. To be a stand-up comic (I've dabbled in it), you've got to be in people's faces. Up there, alone with a mic. Look at me! Listen to me! That's a very masculine endeavor, very tribal, very aggressive. Whatever it is that draws gay men to musical theater, there is a component of stand-up that attracts more, er, sapphic entertainers.

Women don't get fireworks and explosive devices like men do. Firecrackers, M-80's, Roman candles are pyro-erotic for guys. Women are clueless as to the absolute exhilaration experienced over blowing a mailbox apart or lighting an explosive that could blow your hand off. They have no idea what they're missing.

Women are intellectually superior to men. Oh, there may be some studies about math scores or spatial differentiation, but don't kid yourself, women are dangerously intelligent, which makes the premium our society puts on youth especially cruel and stupid. We really have got this one wrong. What's that old saw? Men grow distinguished as they age and women just age? Still, some of us—many of us?—seem to believe this. Just watch TV or skim through a magazine and you will swear that aging is a lethal disease. It's sad. But women, I hate to say, bring so much of this on themselves. They perpetuate the myths and the nonsense, swearing the whole time that men are the genesis of such.

Americans are antediluvian when it comes to women in

politics. Other countries, some thought to be more chauvinistic culturally, have shown no problems with the notion of a woman leader: witness Ségolène Royal of France; Benazir Bhutto of Pakistan; Maggie Thatcher of Great Britain; Indira Gandhi of India; and Golda Meir of Israel. Hillary Clinton faces her biggest hurdles in American politics because of her gender. Despite women's superiority, they're dead meat politically in the U.S.

The only reason for this power differential is that men tended to be able to flatten women initially. Said differential set the course in motion. There is no reason why women shouldn't be in power today. None. And while we're on the subject, this notion of men being stronger than women may be true statistically. But as women have been increasingly athletic over the years, this power difference is becoming increasingly irrelevant and, frankly, untrue.

And yet, women really are emotional basket cases. I'm sorry. And, yes, their periods add vicissitudinal swings to ostensible insanity. And why shouldn't they? My God, when I think of what women go through I don't know how it is that there aren't more female serial killers. We'll get to this point in a sec. But this absolute biological fact should not be a point of derision or ridicule, it is a point that is truly awe-inspiring. If men had periods, businesses would be closed all over the world on any given day. How do women navigate this emotional rollercoaster? And why do we men laugh at them? That being said, I have seen the face of evil and its initials are PMS. Laugh all you want, dismiss me as misogynistic; it's all true. Maybe. I read this on an ad over a urinal in an Irish pub: There are two theories to arguing with women; neither works.

I expect this to royally piss off every woman I know from my inamorata to my sisters to my mother and my editor too, apparently. But what can you expect from broads? That was a joke. But despite what anyone may suggest, the complexities of women (true, sometimes translated into unadulterated insanity) are the basis for what we men see as irrational. Women are Ferraris. What do you expect from something this high-performance?

THE MAN IN THE MOON

We've always been in love with the moon. *Dark Side of the Moon. The Man in the Moon. Moon over Miami. A Moon for the Misbegotten.* Moon watches. Moon boots. "How High the Moon." How High Keith Moon. New moon. Old moon. Half moon. Blue moon. Full moon.

Ah, yes. The full moon. How many times have you heard that *they've* proven that during a full moon there are more emergency room visits, more 911 calls, more crimes, more suicides, more mayhem, more you-name-it than when there's no full moon?

It's automatic.

It's axiomatic.

It's been linked to lycanthropy (just ask Lon Chaney). Ask a lunatic. Ask someone just plain loony.

People swear they've read it. That it's been documented. Just like the Richard Gere gerbil incident. It's true, just ask a bartender. Ask a cop or an EMS technician.

Bullshit.

There is not and has never been a *they,* as in *they've* proven it. The moon is always full, always there. The gravitational effect on you of a mosquito on the arm of the guy next to you at the bar is a million times greater than that of the moon. The Sun's gravitational effect, Brobdingnagian in scope, is always forgotten.

"Yeah, but what about tides?" I hear you say. Well, what *about* tides? The moon affects tides. True. In *open* water systems. Systems that are "boundaryless." Oceans. But the body is 85 percent (whatever the rate is this week) water, and so is the Earth. Sorry, Charlie. The Earth's surface is 85 percent water, i.e., it is covered by water, not *filled* by it.

It matters not this disquisition into the full-moon effect. Let's just say that since the moon is best seen at night and nighttime is when it's dark and that's when shit primarily happens, it may just be the *moon* effect. You see, since day one man has always confused correlation and causation. Maybe a bad event happened when the moon was full eons ago. Forget that it happened at night when we tend not to see as well, when *nocturnal* critters walk about and weird shit happens. Then assume it happened yet again. At night. When the moon was full. There certainly seems to be a correlation, but man wants to go for the big enchilada: the cause. The full moon *caused* the event.

We just love to attribute things happening to something other than the boring reality of randomness. Friday the Thirteenth. People die in threes. Saturday night's all right for fighting. Good-luck charms. The rabbit's foot. Superstition. (Religion?) We just can't help but connect everything with anything, anything with something. Its source is our desire for control and predictability. It's our desire for narrative. It's our desire for a really good cheese.

LIONEL LAW: Women think they look worse than they do; men think they look better.

SEND IN THE CLONES

Now, this is really neat. I know we're not even close to this ever happening, but just think.

Say you clone yourself by taking a human ovum and evacuating the nucleus. You replace it with your DNA, zap it with some electricity, and *voila*! You've theoretically made an embryo—of you. You then implant the embryo and you're born. (Again?) After the birth of you a birth certificate is completed.

Child's name: <u>You</u>

Child's parents: <u>Your parents</u>

Your relationship to the child? _____

Now it gets sticky. It's not your son or daughter nor is it a sibling. It's you.

What legal responsibility do you have for you?

Child support? It's not your child.

Does this clone, er, you, have an ability to take under *your* parents' will? Mind-boggling, indeed.

It gets even better. There used to be a common law rule that said that if a child is born a year or more after the death of a woman's husband, the deceased is presumed not to be the father. It made sense. Gestation periods are roughly nine months. But what about now? Frozen embryos, sperm on ice. Say a very wealthy man dies and his new wife decides to unfreeze some of Daddy Warbucks's sperm and you know the rest. A child is born who, faster than you can say iced latte, seeks to take under his deceased father's will. The geezer's original family objects, claiming that he never would have wanted this. What say you, American law?

And what if DNA is gathered without your consent? Say Mick Jagger is getting his hair cut and an unscrupulous barber grabs some of his hair and is able to extract some of Mick's DNA. Mick's then cloned thereafter. His hair apparent, you might say. What would be the crime or cause of action if there was ever to be one? Wrongful life? (That's actually been used in another context.) Criminal appropriation of a nucleotide? It's, again, mind-boggling.

Granted, we're a long way from this scenario, but not at all when you think of the frozen-sperm scenario.

YOU CAN'T APPEAL AN EXECUTION

Capital punishment is the kiss of death for talk radio audiences. (Very punny.)

And rightfully so.

I've tried for years to find a new angle with which to approach the issue. Something fresh. And I think I've done it. I've found the question that nails my main objection to capital punishment and, I humbly feel, hammers home why it must be abolished *in toto*. (Nothing to do with Dorothy's little dog, in case you're wondering.)

Here goes: How many erroneous executions would you permit before you once and for all demanded the abolition of the death penalty, or at least a moratorium?

It's a simple enough question.

The answer may be a little harder to come by.

Some legal scholars estimate that more than 100 death-row exonerations have occurred since the Supreme Court reinstated the death penalty in 1976. Gee, just over 100. That's not *that* much, is it? Actually you thought there would be more, right?

Really?

Not that much?

You thought there'd be more?

Tell that to the more than 100—repeat, more than 100—who have been *exonerated*. The more than 100 who would have been executed had not some sanity, some reconsideration been applied. More than 100 names with families and lives and futures who would have been extinguished and expunged.

Oops.

Stop for a second. How many people do you know? Could that number be 100? Imagine all of those friends executed. Innocently. And why there's even a debate astounds me to no end.

Think about this carefully.

Is there a number of wrongfully executed humans that you would tolerate before you'd demand death-penalty abolition? Okay, maybe you wouldn't miss the guy at the mini-mart who always seems to shortchange you or that snooty barista (or anyone for that matter who refers to himself as a barista) who serves you that four-dollar cup of coffee.

And maybe you're not too crazy about your brother-in-law. And let's face it, you don't find too many Mensa members or yachting aficionados on death row. And you sure as hell don't find any first offenders; if they didn't do this murder, believe you me, they did something else and probably weren't caught. But c'mon, you've got to admit that capital punishment is a pretty extreme solution. In fact, it's as extreme as you can get.

But who knows? You may be so in love with the notion of state-sanctioned murder that any number of erroneous executions would be okeydokey. The cost of doing business. You know, to make an omelet you have to break a few eggs. No system's perfect, right? If you're one of these clowns, I feel for your family.

The reasons that the death penalty should be abolished are pretty straightforward even without the higher issue of the morality of taking a life through state-sanctioned revenge.

Consider this: It seems that every week defendants sentenced to prison (in nonmurder cases for the most part) are released, vindicated, and exonerated when DNA shows them to be innocent. It's commonplace. So commonplace it's buried on Page 15. No big deal. Sad. It's usually a black man who's been warehoused for decades. He thanks his lawyers, thanks God, tries to move on and recapture those missing years, as if he could. Forget for a moment that he left a country awash in eight-track tapes and now tries to find his place in the land of iPods.

The problem is, DNA isn't even a factor in a lot of capital cases. Defendants are convicted on the words of jailhouse snitches. Losers so jammed up they'll say anything to catch a break. These losers are responsible for an inordinate proportion of capital-case evidence. An accomplice, perhaps. Bad eyewitnesses. Coerced confessions. Yep, DNA's great but it ain't necessarily helpful in capital cases.

Did I say coerced confessions? Sure did. My new friend, you'd be amazed at the number of absolutely innocent people that have caved in to incessant and unreasonable police questioning and have confessed to something they didn't do. I can't explain why. It amazed me when I first heard about it as a legal tyro. But it happens more than you can imagine. Many jurisdictions have adopted new procedures for taking statements and confessions that include videotaping all interrogations and the like. That should help. But how are we to trust the legitimacy and accuracy of a confession? OK, they're not all contaminated or coerced, but do you really want to execute people based on them? You'd take a chance?

Remember, you can't appeal an execution.

I guess it's the finality of death (did I just say that?) that should eliminate the death penalty from consideration by all sentient people. But that's not enough for many. They've a fetish about execution. I swear, it's almost sexual. By God, no one is taking away their death penalty. No one. Why, it's American. And while we share the distinction of having a death penalty with some of the most brutal regimes in the world, and while Western civilization has abolished the brutality of state-sanctioned murder, to many in this country—who cares?

The death penalty is about revenge, plain and simple. It's about making that son-of-a-bitch pay the ultimate price. An eye for an eye. Quid pro quo. But what I simply don't comprehend is how those revenge-seekers fail to realize that "nighty night" by needle is a cakewalk compared to being warehoused for the rest of your life. They'd rot. Their existence would be inhuman. Think of it. The rest of your life. Never to see or taste freedom. Never. And don't give me this Club Fed business or these imaginary prisons that people speak of with cable TV. *Emeril* reruns in no wise satisfy a person's natural desire for freedom. It's a fate worse than death and, frankly, I see not why the revengers don't insist upon it.

How many erroneous executions would you allow? Remember, that's the question.

Now when I get someone to reconsider their bloodlust and death penalty obsession, they will normally respond with a version of "Well, what if we limit the death penalty to be used against those who really, really are guilty? One hundred percent. What about then?" There goes that adherence to the death penalty. They won't budge from their love of it.

The response is simple. In every case where a defendant was later acquitted or exonerated, the case was 100 percent.

In every case where a confession was thrown out by an appellate court or an eyewitness's testimony was discredited or invalidated, the case was seen as case closed. To use the Tenetian reference: a slam dunk. There were juries, prosecutors, defense lawyers, trial judges, appellate courts. Each reviewed the case in its entirety. Yet despite these procedural safeguards, innocent people were convicted and sentenced to death. There can simply be no 100 percent certain. Yeah, but what about Ted Bundy, John Wayne Gacy, Timothy McVeigh? There was no doubt in anyone's mind of their guilt. What about executing them? Nope. It's all or nothing. You can't permit the death penalty at all if you want to prevent erroneous executions. For every high-profile case, there's some poor schmuck on trial in Armpit, Louisiana, who is every bit as innocent as he claims to be. So long as the death penalty exists, there will be erroneous executions. Again. Death penalty proponents say there's no proof that an innocent person was ever executed, but ask yourself. Come on. We've released scores of innocent men from prison, men who'd been incarcerated for years, and you mean to tell me that when it comes to the death penalty, we're thorough and accurate in the assessment of guilt? Puh-leeze.

You can't appeal an execution.

Another aspect of the problem is that there are so few cases even eligible for the death penalty. Murders for the most part. First degree, at that. There aren't that many cases where execution is even available. It's only for the really heinous. And, oh yeah, are they heinous. When people see crime scene photos for the first time, they are shocked at the inhumanity and savagery of that dirt bag who the state says did this. When they see the decomposed remains of a child or a very bloody crime scene, the anger surges and that primordial instinct of revenge takes over. And who could blame them?

I'll never forget the color photos I saw as a young prosecutor. It seems a woman was attacked while she slept with her lover by her machete-wielding estranged husband. The photos were absolutely incredible. I had never seen anything like it. I remember she was almost beheaded. Her tongue was thrusting out almost mockingly. The repeated machete blows on her back showed me for the first time adipose tissue; it looked like chicken fat. Blood was everywhere. Think about it. If you've ever donated a pint of blood, that's just a pint. No big deal. You feel fine afterward. If I were to take that mere pint and spread it around, you'd think there had been a bloodbath. Just imagine what five liters would look like. That's how much blood is in the human body.

To be sure, when jurors see firsthand the handiwork of somebody charged with first-degree murder, it's all they can do not to leap out of their jury box and strangle the bastard. And in every case where a defendant was wrongfully convicted of murder and shuttled off to death row, some jury saw similar pictures and heard the howls of parents and relatives mourning the tragic loss of a loved one.

But you can't appeal an execution.

Then there's the issue of how the death penalty is apportioned. You've read the statistics showing that blacks are disproportionately exposed to the death penalty. Black-on-white crime is treated differently than the reverse. Poor, African-American, Latino: you're SOL, baby. There is absolutely a different system and a double standard. So often judges have appointed lawyers who are not experienced in capital cases. You've heard of lawyers showing up to court drunk or falling asleep. Court-appointed lawyers and public defenders along with legal-aid lawyers are outspent by the prosecution, which has all the bucks when it comes to securing convictions. If an indigent defendant's lawyer wants to hire private investigators, serologists, or jury consultants, or wants DNA testing conducted, he's ofttimes limited by a statutory cap for investigative costs. Remember, the state has all the resources it needs to get its man. There is no indigent version of the FBI lab. I know that on the hierarchy of objections, a defendant's not receiving a fair trial doesn't even register with many people. So the trial wasn't fair; he's still guilty, right? Folks in our country have been told that the jails and prisons are a revolving door and are filled with guilty monsters who take advantage of the system with baseless and warrantless appeals quibbling and trifling over criminal-procedure minutiae. So, who cares if a guilty person didn't receive a fair trial? When it comes to abecedarian jurisprudence and legal fundamentals, our citizens are bereft of basic understanding and appreciation for the significance of these protections.

The least persuasive argument against the death penalty is often dismissed as the bleeding-heart analysis, the liberal blather. So be it. But there's something so sickening about seeing our country's citizens wring their hands in a ghoulish, bloodthirsty, fang-bearing glee whenever someone is executed. We lose something collectively, for we're no better than the louse who's being exterminated. I feel nothing for anyone who has brutally taken someone's life. And when there's a child involved, I see red. I want the killer dead, expunged, erased from the world. And then I calm down and realize that my behavior, my rage, while justified, reduces me to the level of the animal on trial. There are some people in the world that are devoid of humanity. They are hybrids: unfeeling, sociopathic animals who weren't in school the day compassion was taught. I can't believe they share DNA with me. But what if the victim was your kid? This is the "gotcha" refrain that death-penalty proponents love to zing you with. Well, of course, it goes without saying that if a family member of mine was brutally raped and murdered I'd prefer the killer face torture of medieval proportions. A torture so hideous and prolonged it would shock the conscience of Vlad the Impaler himself. Of course I'd feel that way. I'd want to perform the torture myself. But that example is unrealistic. Anyone who says they'd love to pull the switch is so septically full of shit. Big talk. Barstool diplomacy. There is something that makes us human that we sometimes forget. There is an instinct, an organic aversion to killing other humans. It's inherent in us and atavistic. Combat veterans have described the killing of anonymous strangers to be at times worse than seeing comrades who've fallen. When we clamor for death and cheer on the execution of a subhuman, we lose something. We lose part of our collective souls.

Not to mention, you can't appeal an execution.

IT NEVER RAINS, BUT IT POURS

Noah gets the word from God that he has to build an ark because Big Daddy is going to flood the Earth for forty days and nights. If you don't swim or fly and you're not on that ark, sayonara, adios, auf Wiedersehen, arrivederci, adieu to you and you and you. Male and female pairs of every species must be on that ark or there will be extinction to pay.

Now, let's see about this whopper.

The volume of rain that would have to fall per second for that forty day and forty night period is, let's just say, pretty significant. Millions of gallons per second. Enough to cover mountains—Everest, Kilimanjaro, Space Mountain at Disney World. At least enough so that water levels would be high enough to soak to death any life that would be at such levels. After all, God's not prone to overkill.

That's some rainfall.

Then again, this is God and God can do anything.

Every species to live after the flood and after the waters recede (and that's another issue altogether) must have been on that ark. Everything. That means *a fortiori* that Noah and the kids had some serious animal-collection chores. Male and female, fertile and ready to multiply for future's sake, on that ark. Camels, lions, rhinoceroses, baboons, snakes, aardvarks, lemurs, kitty cats, puppy dogs, goldfish, Republicans. They all had to be on that ark.

In fact, any animal species you see today would necessarily have been on that ark for the idea of them evolving independently since the flood and recession would be impossible. Postdiluvian development of, say, the polar bear? Wait. The polar bear. Wouldn't the polar bear, for example, have had to be on the ark? And if so, where did Noah and his kids find *two*? Not to mention exotic baboons, spider monkeys, marmosets, lemurs, capuchins, gorillas.

Now after the flood and its recession, Noah and his family found a world barren. Silt, muck, and myriad shit must have been strewn about. Dead bodies would have been seen. The scene must have been rife with putrefaction, decay, typhoid, God knows what. (Literally.) We're not talking about the stadium after the big game. There wouldn't be any paper cups, beer bottles, or Styrofoam containers. And there wouldn't have been anybody there. Nobody. No body, that is, save Noah and his kids. The world had to repopulate from that point forward with what was available, again, Noah and his kids.

So I ask you.

Where do the Koreans come from?

FROM YOUR ASS TO MY EARS

The necessary downside and drawback to any form of communication is the unintended and erroneous transmission. The oops factor. The wrong number. The misfire. The wrong address. (Imagine the problems with smoke signals.) And it's funny that I rarely get a wrong number either via land line or cell phone. The historically wrong number, that is. A misdialed digit, a stranger mistakenly talking to me.

But then there's the *nouveau* "booty call." Not a wrong number *per se*, but an unintended one.

Here's the scenario. The phone rings and caller ID may have provided the caller's name, say, your editrix. What is heard is a long and uninterrupted muffled jumble of . . . nothing.

She's sat on her cell phone or BlackBerry and accidentally

called you. A phenomenon brought to you by advances in telecommunications. Al Bell never thought of this after the Mr. Watson bit.

Sometimes the message is not so muffled. Sometimes the call is very, er, embarrassingly clear. And do you listen in? Or do you respect the privacy of your friend and hang up on this unintended, accidental call?

Hell no! You listen to it in its entirety. And then you save it.

THE LUCK OF THE IRISH PUB

The Irish are to bars what Kenyans are to marathons.

They are simply the best.

Period.

They have an absolute understanding of the boozer. They're not judgmental and know no recrimination. Most of the time, their own private guzzling dwarfs anything you can even think of besting. And I say that with all due respect. I'm not suggesting that all alcoholics are Irish, no, wait, not that all Irish are . . . look, who cares? I love these grand and brilliant people and thank their God for who they are. Great, grand, and wonderful people. That being said . . .

Everyone should have an Irish pub. The real McCoy. An Irish pub with real Irish. It's McNirvana. There's nothing that I can speak to that nails the Irish bar. The long mahogany bar, Guinness taps. An actual Irishman behind the stick. Yeah, I guess that's it, in part. But it's more than that.

> **LIONEL LAW:** Never refer to an Irish accent as a *brogue*. A brogue is a shoe.

Make no mistake about it, the Irish have no accent. *You* do. These "accents" can be doozies and absolutely indecipherable. To us. We're not talking Barry Fitzgerald here. One way to tell when you're absolutely waxed? The Irish bartender starts to make sense. Now, don't get me wrong, I love these people. But I've heard gutturals and gasps that are absolutely impossible to understand. But I love them. Not only are they the greatest hosts of hootch ever, but when a buyback is commenced at a good Irish joint the bartender will either knuckle-knock the bar (as in knocking on a door) or say "good luck" or a combination. It doesn't get any better than that.

Never ask an Irish bartender where he's from. Don't tell him you were in Ireland once. Don't tell him your old grandpappy was from Cork. And DON'T tell him you're Irish. You're an American. A narrowback at best. They're Irish. Got it? And they've got the best bars in the world, bar none.

WORDS FAIL ME

What's happening to our language?

We're devolving is what's happening.

We're sliding into a morass of verbal, grammatic, and linguistic ignorance and it's getting worse and coming at us from all directions.

Take "like," please. Take it and destroy it. Almost overnight, "like" has become ubiquitous, especially by mindnumbed adolescents and young 'uns who seem to punctuate every pause or break in a sentence with it. If there's one law I'd love to pass it's the mandatory caning of anyone caught using "like" more than four times in a single sentence. Who started this? Well, Moon Zappa introduced us to "Valleyspeak" and it caught on like a virus.

It's a pandemic.

At least she was a kid. What excuse is there for George W. Bush, our cacoepist-in-chief, who has made "nucular" acceptable? Instead of inspiring criticism, he was seen as quaint and unpretentious. He's a symbol of what's happened to our speech. And whenever I bring this up, I'm told that Jimmy Carter pronounced it the same way. Who cares? Then Jimmy Carter's a dolt also.

What's happening to us?

When the "internets" (thanks again, Dubya) came about and emailing and texting and IM'ing followed, I stupidly and mistakenly thought that, finally, words would mean something again. That our style of writing would take on a new cachet, that people would appreciate that since we're actually writing, we'd take care to spruce up our grammar and writing style. What was I thinking? Email and texting have brought us "How R U 2day?" Yikes! And we're not talking about pimple-faced kids, adults view this as shorthand. Shorthand?! It's getting worse. When I've brought this up before on the air or among friends, I felt that I was being perceived as pedantic and priggish, an unnecessarily haughty stickler for technical correctness and the like. There's nothing nitpicky about expecting people to exhibit rudimentary language skills.

Let me give an example that still cracks me up. Have you ever worked in an office setting where interoffice email and memos just spew from certain coworkers? I was in such an institution where this one memo writer was a gem. I couldn't wait for her new pronouncements and declarations. They were priceless. Seems that this nice lady would merely spell-check her handiwork and failed to recognize the separate category for grammar, punctuation, and the like. She once implored us to keep a door closed and thanked us for our "corporations." When informing us that windows would be cleaned, she instructed us to remove personal effects from the window "seal." When the FCC was cracking down on naughty and prohibited speech on the radio, she demanded that we refrain from using "ex-rated" language. What? Language that was rated at one time? Ex-president, ex-wife? Ex-rated? When I brought that to her attention, she looked as though I was speaking Esperanto. In fact, maybe that was the problem. Maybe she did.

Spell-check is great, except when it's not. Unfortunately, it not homophonic. (Not that there's anything wrong with that.) Do you say what you mean and mean what you say? Do you mean this? Or do you mean that?

This	That	(Or the Other?)
there	their	they're
blue	blew	
here	hear	
chews	choose	

This	That	(Or the Other?)
no	know	no no no *(only if you're* *Amy Winehouse)*
rain	rein	reign
to	too	two

Don't let this happen to ewe!

Which brings me to ew! The exclamation point is used constantly, especially by women who think it means "I really mean it." Happy Birthday! I love you! Why was she exclaiming and screaming such? It means not what people think. Why the expression of surprise, anger, or pain? I know, I know, I'm wasting my time. There's no choir to preach to. Except you, of course.

Slang, accents, patois, regionalism, that's all fine and good. I would hate to think of an homogenized, universal American. Imagine no Southern twang, no Brooklyn, no Boston, no Ha-vahd Yahd. Perish the thought. But we're collectively rejecting the rudiments, the fundamentals of our speech, and we're losing it.

It tickles me whenever the illegal immigration debate (translation: Mexicans) arises and language tests are proposed. Or when English is proposed as the official language subject to enforcement. Enforcement?! Hell, the President of the United

States couldn't speak English. What level of proficiency would anyone consider as being the baseline for English-speaking? Remember when some folks suggested years ago the establishment of Ebonics as a legitimate language or speaking style or whatever? That was laughed out of any rational discussion. But think of someone trying that in France. This goes to show you that as with manners and etiquette, the correct speaking of *our* language is looked at as a needless trifling.

And then there's those internets again.

POSSESSION IS NINE-TENTHS
OF THE LAW

I have to speak of my absolutely favorite religious construction and the cartoon character to end all cartoon characters.

Satan.

Beelzebub.

Mephistopheles.

The Prince of Darkness.

Lucifer.

Ol' What's His Face.

As a kid I was the Devil every Halloween. I loved this cat. Horned, goateed, red, with a pitchfork no less. Then there was that barbed tail. And, oh yeah, he was caped. You can't make this stuff up. Or did they? Hollywood loved this character; the movies are countless. My favorite was, of course, *The Exorcist*. The notion of possession was sheer brilliance.

What a great way to disguise mental illness or personify in-explicable evil. When the devil was enjoying an incarnation as himself, say in *Devil's Advocate*, he was a deliciously creepy guy, swarthy and smarmy . . . and usually a lawyer. How about De Niro in *Angel Heart* as Lou Cyphre? (Get it? Luci-fer?) But I've always had these questions and observations about El Diablo. And there's nothing wrong with asking questions. Ever. If the Devil is as big a badass as they claim, he must be a very clever cat to have terrorized so many for so long.

Some questions are in order:

When the devil decides to possess someone, why not the President of the United States? (All right, you're thinking, what about Dubya? Is he possessed? Come on, the Devil is by nature smart and he wouldn't besmirch his carefully se-lected possessed person for that dumb shit.) No, it was al-ways some little girl in Venezuela or some poor schlub who happened to be suffering from mental illness. Gee, maybe it wasn't the devil, but rather a misunderstood element and symptom of his dementia?

Do you think?

When the Devil did possess some hapless kid, why did he call so much attention to himself? You know, the split pea emesis, the incessant expletives. Your mother darns socks in hell! (An old joke, admittedly.) What was the purpose of this? Why call attention to yourself? Why not remain dormant for a while so that you can kind of get a lay of the land? Hasn't the Devil ever heard of going undercover? I think you can cause more harm and spread more Devil shit by lying low. And what could this eight-year-old possibly do that the Devil couldn't by possessing someone else by slightly more subtle means? Look, asking these questions is like asking why nobody ever killed Gilligan after he screwed up so many chances to leave that uncharted isle. I know this. But if there's a Devil, don't you think she'd be smarter?

Why, when the Devil speaks through the exorcist, does his speech sound eerily Tarzan-African? You know, that mumbo jumbo faux African that the "natives" always screamed on *Tarzan* episodes. If he doesn't sound like some Johnny Weissmuller foil (or actually, like Johnny Weissmuller himself . . . see, I didn't mention Arnold), he sounds like a kidnapper, circa *Columbo* 1972. I can just picture it now, Beelzebub in an office with broadloom and pendant lamps, speaking into a harvest gold telephone with a handkerchief wrapped around the receiver, demanding two million in unmarked bills or else the kid gets it.

That prompts an interesting question. Why does the devil never demand anything? No souls, no followers. He proselytizes no one in the least. He wants nothing. No money, nothing. He rarely even mentions your soul anymore. Where's the tenacity of the Mormons or Jehovah's Witnesses? They come door to door and want to sell you . . . something. That

Watchtower magazine. Salvation. Why can't he match that? Furthermore, he promises nothing. No pretty girl, no house on the hill, no Cadillac Escalade. Not even an iPod. What's that all about? I mean, what's his motivation? What the hell does this guy want?

Speaking of tenacity (we were, weren't we?), it apparently takes nothing to get him to scoot. A Bible verse here and there, some holy water, and the persistent demand to leave. That's it?! Just ask him to leave and that's it? Vamoose, El Diablo. OK, I'm leaving. My Aunt Betty won't leave that easily. Dammit! What kind of an archetypal bad guy is this? At least Dracula needed some garlic and light and a stake through his heart. That was a bad mutha. The Devil's a wimp.

Why in the name of God would God let this character keep his magical powers upon being bounced from Heaven? OK, maybe it's akin to Grant letting Lee's men keep their horses, but certainly not their guns. Can we expect more from the inebriate Grant than God? Evict the son of a bitch but cut his balls off. Is this too much to expect from God? And when Saint Michael the Archangel (whatever the hell that is) tossed Lucifer out, why not complete the job?

The Vatican has its own Department of Exorcisms (or something), which I imagine to be something like the Department of Motor Vehicles, without the lines. Now that must be some Christmas party. They believe in the Devil and exorcisms. Fine. How come other faiths missed this nec-essary branch of their hierarchy? Seems like the Devil has a thing against Catholics. Why? Likely it has something to do with tartan uniforms and patent leather shoes.

Let's get real, shall we?

I have a sneaky suspicion that millennia ago whilst man was rather maladroit at spotting things like, oh, say, schizo-phrenia, maybe, just maybe, he might have thought that someone in the throes of going batshit might be possessed by something, oh, I don't know, evil, maybe. How many poor crazy people were tended to by having demons cast out ver-sus an IV drip of Thorazine? OK, fine. That was then. But now? You mean that somewhere in the hierarchy of possible causes for weird behavior an educated priest would jump to the conclusion of possession over a psychotic fit?

And how is a potential exorcism candidate screened for mental unfitness? Are there questions and answers? Sir, your name, please. Date of birth. Insurance carrier? Have you ever experienced your head spinning at the shoulder before? And your levitation?

Just curious.

NOTE OF THE FOOT:

I was interviewing a religious zealot—sorry, that's unfair. A religious nut! I read a passage of his book—I won't say which one—which detailed how he believed in God, prayed to God, tithed in the name of God and, get this, worried (worried!) that he may love his wife and kids more than God. I looked at him askance and he looked back quizzically. What's wrong with that? His devotion to God. His words. I then had an idea. What if I replaced "God" with "Bob" in the chap's book.

Try it for yourself. Reread the preceding paragraph and replace "God" with "Bob." See?

Case closed.

Your witness.

LIONEL LAW: The reason why we've sunk so low as to pigeonhole politics solely according to the lib vs. con stratum is that we are pathetically ignorant as to the real issues. We eschew complexity and end up with this silly labeling. I will remain neutral on this, only stopping to note again that I hate conservatives.

NO SANE MAN WILL DANCE

No truer words were ever spoken.

Thank you, Marcus Tullius Cicero.

I have used incessantly the concepts of atavism and primordial behavior throughout this exercise in bookdom. I appreciate that there are things that humans inherently do that make them human. We are the only species to enjoy language. Sure, I know there are the dolphin- and chimp-lovers who will point to communication, but that's not language. Language is ours, as is typing, driving, and eating sushi.

Humans if left to their own devices will invariably develop language, song, theater, poetry, sports, competition, and . . . dance. Dance. It should be a four-letter word. Really, it's the silliest thing that we do. And when men do it, it's even sillier. I'm not talking of the balletic among us, those acrobats like

Baryshnikov and Nureyev who soar across the stage. (By the way: A ballerina is a female ballet dancer. A male ballet dancer is called a danseur or a *ballerino*. Just thought you'd like to know.) And I'm not talking of the John Travoltas and the Michael Jacksons who sway and gyrate with an almost unnatural ability. They can syncopate movement, traveling through time and space in a way that seems to defy several of the laws of physics. These guys all possess(ed) a supernatural ability to move poetically. I marvel at their talents. I bow before their greatness. They are the Beethovens of the ballet world, the Jobims of movement. I am in awe of them.

Ahhhh.

What I despise is a different sort of male dancer, the pathetic white guy who feels some duty to attempt the sway. With his classic overbite, a Giuliani comb-over, and finger-snapping that signals an arrhythmic rhythm, this character makes me retch. He's a testament to neurological dysfunction, an out-of-sync, out-of-step, mindless gyrator whose sole intention is to attract the female. What female worth getting could and would be lured by such flailings, I just don't know.

True, I singled out the Caucasoid hoofer. Am I racist? If so, who cares? Am I self-loathing? Hardly, for I care not to dance. At least I care not to dance *at* a woman but rather *with* her.

White men can't jump and they can't dance either. I am not saying all black men can, but for some reason thinking of them doesn't inspire the degree of hilarity that white men dancing inspires in me. Or maybe I haven't seen many black men dance. Or maybe I've just been looking in a mirror. Whatever.

What I'm talking about is the observation that is causing you to nod in an almost hypnotic approbation. You know exactly what I'm talking about. Admit it.

I'm speaking of the almost inarticulable disgust I feel when I see the worst white dancer of all time, Hugh Hefner, slog about. This man, whom I admire for many obvious reasons, decided at some time in his life that the *Playboy* lifestyle includes some hoary schlepper jerking about. Hugh Hefner "dances" as though both of his feet are cast in concrete. He flails and attempts to groove.

What in the name of God compels men who've perhaps had a nip or three to swirl about with a bellyful of warm Scotch? Maybe I wasn't in school that day. Maybe I missed the whole bit. But somebody help me with the concept.

White men, especially those in the throes of decrepitude, should not be go-going on the dance floor, snapping their fingers and gesticulating in some Saint Vitus's dance fugue. It's ballism revisited. It's pathetic, sad, and should be outlawed.

What possesses this man to think that such is attractive or even good? What must he be thinking? Neurologists have fought to rid humankind of chorea and Sydenhamlike maladies. Why do white guys think that mimicking such to a disco beat is attractive, seductive, or within the bounds of decency?

And you look gay. That's right. If you dance too well, you look gay. I'm not going to state the obligatory *Seinfeld* retort, but no, I find nothing wrong with being gay. However, there is that risk if you're not. Looking gay while trying to attract a gal is not a good thing and, frankly, is counterproductive. Gay men and women are naturally good dancers. This is a fact.

Men, ask yourselves, do you really want to dance? Honestly, are you motivated by some need to enjoy music through a tribal ritual that disgusts me? No, probably not. You've most probably been duped into looking profoundly retarded by some woman who has told you she loves to dance. You know the drill, brothers. "I love to dance. Do you?" And sure as shit, you respond with the mindless "Of course." Don't fall for this. No, this is not some prehistoric vestige of an instinct that permits the young lass to correlate your dance moves with your worth as a husband or mate. In all probability, she's lugging you onto the dance floor so that she can show off her perceived moves, thereby attracting a new suitor, while you, a submental Bobby Burgess, look like a damn fool.

Bugs dance to attract a mate. They can't ply some grub worm with chardonnay and lie like the rest of us. They have to dance. Do you think they like the exhaustion? They dance because they *have* to.

You don't.

Buy her a bottle of wine and call it a day.

That's what a sane man does.

I DIDN'T STEAL IT, I FOUND IT.

The law is just great when it comes to the obvious, e.g., robbery, credit card theft, mopery (my favorite). But technology has brought about more nuanced issues. American jurisprudence reacts to something and never anticipates it. It catalogues human behavior and comes up with new ways to prohibit certain examples of such. But technological advances give new problems to the lawmaker.

Consider file sharing.

With the advent of file sharing and peer-to-peer distribution, the music industry doesn't know what hit it. Intellectual property law is already antiquated because it never anticipated—nor could it have—the Internet.

Let me clarify.

The laws are great when it comes to trademarks,

copyrights, and patents. They're still in effect. But the law never imagined that songs, music, movies, and the like would be disseminated and distributed virally with the click of a mouse. (No, this is *not* artificial dissemination.)

What many don't get—those of us over twenty, for example—is that a great number of people fail to see how sharing a song can be construed as stealing. This boggles their mind. Their computer is the portal to an open domain where everything's free and open. Free and open. That's a good thing, right? That means free and open for us, right? Stealing, well, stealing means breaking into a shop. A stocking over your face. Stick 'em up. You know, stealing, robbery, larceny.

But some feel that this music was "found." It's right there. And if I don't get it, someone else will. What's the big deal?

You want an exercise in futility? Try explaining to a twenty-something that taking a song without paying for it is stealing. That it's an appropriation of someone's creative effort. Good luck. I'd rather explain the benefits of abstinence to a horn-dog teenage boy. I know I sound like an old fart (because I am) but today's *yutes* have no inherent ability to understand the nuanced aspects of a creative endeavor being protected and paid for when used.

But is it? The kid knows that there are fair use exceptions to copyright laws. He certainly can burn a copy of an album or CD for himself after he's purchased it. At least, he thinks you can. Besides, who's going to know? One copy for a friend.

Big deal.

Now switch the scenario somewhat. Instead of one copy make it two million. That's what happens instantaneously on the Internet. Some schmuck writes a song, sells one copy of it, two million are shared, and he's now the proud writer of a Number One hit that nobody's purchased. Meanwhile the law says "Doh!"

HERE COMES THE $26,327 PARTY

Weddings. They're the Super Bowl of the courtship ritual. The World Series of Dating. The most idiotic ceremony and rite that we as humans—no, correct that—that *women* engage in. Weddings are anachronistic, outdated, and just stupid. Antediluvian, atavistic, vestigial. I mean, there is really nothing that we do as humans, and let's be frank here (yet again), I can only speak for Americans, that is so off-the-charts nuts as weddings. The prototypical wedding, that is.

And if there was ever evidence and indicia of the outer-space mentality of the American lass, it's right here.

You see, it is so often and too often the case that women are overheard repeating that psychotic refrain of always dreaming of that special day. The day when the woman is sacrificed and delivered to a man.

The day.

The man.

The one.

What should really be considered a harrowing and bestial rite is camouflaged by the artificial pomp and great expense of a ceremony that makes *American Idol* seem like a Tupperware party. Women dream—DREAM, mind you—of that day. Not the rites, not the vows, not the responsibility, not the forever life-changing event, but the day. The day of their wedding.

The first one, at least.

Now, lest you think ill of me, let me clarify some points. I am a firm believer in love and commitment. No kidding. I'm a softy and a romantic (I swear!) where the notions of commitment and happily ever after are concerned. Marriage is a solemn rite that has been diluted by the likes of no-fault divorce, the Las Vegas chapel wedding, Elizabeth Taylor, Britney Spears, and ice sculptures. It's so sad that few people entering into the bonds of matrimony truly believe it's forever. Because deep within the recesses of their own minds and world experience is the understanding that if things get tough, there's a way out. 'Til death do us part?!

Bullshit.

I completely dig the legal ramifications of marriage:

Tenancy by the entireties.

Special equity.

Pretermitted spouse.

Alimony.

Maintenance.

Chicken Pot Pie.

Look, this isn't a legal treatise (not much), but let me simply say that there are critical considerations that spouses-to-be should understand. Marriage is by analogy the construction of Siamese twins, initially separate. *Per tout et non per moi.* One of the most beautiful or frightening legal concepts ever envisaged by man. "For the whole and not the moiety (half)." Dig. The new entity of the matrimonial estate or *res* is an amalgam that only exists in the formation of marriage. It has no corollary or counterpart. Two people are now adhered together. And should that coalescence break, shatter, or crumble, as in the case of separating conjoined twins, someone's going to make out better than the other. Someone is going to get the good kidney, and someone else will likely die. And guess who that's going to be? Chang or Eng? The groom is more often than not the chump, the victim.

But I digress.

Now let's look at this ceremony, shall we? Let's further dissect what is being portrayed and what is actually happening.

The white gown thing is a great starting point. It's unnecessary to explain the historical juxtaposition of white with virginity, so I won't. But come on! Brides, virginal?! What century are we in, anyway? Unless you're some proto-typical jihadist who has been promised virgins in the hereafter, who would want a virgin bride in the first place? Think about it. Some chick screaming in the bathroom for Mommy while shmucko waits for naught in a heart-shaped bed. (And al Qaeda's promising seventy-two of them, no less. Or was that a seventy-two-year-old virgin?) Not to mention, at any given wedding, there has to be at least one cat in the audience who's tagged Princess Leia.

And the gown itself. First, I have to say that the gown signifies pomp and artificially creates the notion that the event at which the gown is worn is of notable significance. Ball gowns. Evening gowns. Wedding gowns. They know no corollary in male apparel. Not even the tux compares. Nope, the gown is special. Kings and queens wear gowns. And, of course, there's the dressing gown, which I haven't used for years. But I digress. The wedding gown. Now let me get this straight. A woman buys an expensive dress that she will wear ONE TIME?! Let me repeat, ONE TIME?! The only things that we ever use or wear once are normally disposable items, and they are disposable for good reasons. Let's see: condoms, surgical gloves, adult diapers (I really prefer Depends). Hazmat suits are reused, for Chrissake.

But think about it.

The wedding gown is the only, repeat, *only* piece of apparel that is used once and then stored for posterity, never again to be worn save for that daughter who likewise will wear it once and hermetically seal it up yet again. It knows no equal. As if that weren't enough, while she wears a three-thousand-dollar dress, the schlub groom RENTS a tuxedo, a suit he will invariably wear at least once again before (or after) he dies. And his supposed closest buddies? You'd think they'd spend just a little bit more for a basic tux they'd probably wear at least once in their remaining lives. No, they rent. This is absolutely insane.

To make matters worse, the bride selects her bridesmaids (yeah, right, *maids*), who must also purchase a hideous monstrosity that, yes, you guessed it, they will wear ONE TIME! A poofy dress of a color that doesn't exist in nature. A color found nowhere in the visible spectrum. Truly, the colors of bridesmaid dresses are nothing short of amazing in their sickening complexity. Let's see. Chartreuse. Sea foam. Sea foam? Isn't that white, the foam of the sea, that is? And as for white, *which* white? No, there's no such thing as white anymore. There's eggshell white, off-white, pearl, cream, ivory, magnolia, bianco, cosmic latte (I'm not kidding), old lace, cloud, albion, a whiter shade of pale (I just threw that in to mess with you). Of course white is still usually reserved for the virgin bride, so the bridesmaids (the bride's cleaning ladies?) get to wear green. Mint green. Asparagus. Harlequin. Pear. Spring Bud. Tea Green. Olive. Olive you too. Want blue? How about mitochondrial blue. Yale blue. Pale blue. Rail blue. Periwinkle blue. Cornflower blue. Columbia blue. Russian blue. Want something different? How about jaundiced yellow. Dyspeptic green. I suggest the color nausea. It just says it all. Bile. Phlegm, perhaps. You get the picture. Still, no matter what the color, you know that the design is going to be bad. Way bad. 1986 big hair and shoulders bad. A dress of a design that screams: "Hey, look at the crap I had to buy. THAT I WILL NEVER WEAR AGAIN!"

And then there are the parties. The bride has a shower or series of showers. S.H.O.W.E.R. Hmm. When I first heard of the shower, I just imagined a bunch of gals sitting around and throwing a few back. Or maybe some towel-snapping. You know, like men would. But no. From what I've learned from second-hand accounts, the bridal shower is a formalized ceremony that knows no comparison in the real world. You have to go to the jungles of Papua New Guinea or watch *National Geographic* television to really get a handle on the flavor of this absolutely bizarre practice. I thought people were kidding when I first heard of the festivities, and I use that term loosely.

Try this on for size: the ribbon hat. The bride-to-be's best friend collects all the bows and ribbons from gifts received and crafts a makeshift hat from a paper plate. I kid you not. As if that weren't bad enough, there's the food. Sandwiches, for instance. Sandwiches are deconstructed and decrusted to the most basic and minimalistic. They look like something you'd see at the Museum of Modern Art, and not in the museum restaurant. No Dagwoods or heroes for these gals.

Bridal shower "games" are played. Games that don't remotely involve or include fun or base amusement. Symbolic gestures of God knows what. Women don't even know why they're doing this. It's something that must be done and is perhaps the oddest rite humans engage in next to joining the Junior League.

The thematic constant is WELCOME. Welcome, young bride. Welcome to the bride's world. Look! China, crystal, chafing dishes—items of cutlery and dining that you'll never use again lest they be chipped. Again, the theme of the never-again-to-be-used/worn purchase. Silly, idiotic, inane. What is really happening here is a centuries-old ceremony wherein the bride is primed and primped for her new duties as wife. It's been called the hyperfeminization of the woman. It goes back to the days of the dowries and trousseaux. Remember the hope chest? I don't either. Men, I can't even begin to understand this; don't even try. I haven't the foggiest idea why this symbolic event takes place. All I know is that it is expected, it is tradition, and a woman is not to be denied this. They're hardwired for this rite. And that's that.

Now the groom has his bachelor party—maybe.

Let me give a bit of advice to anyone even considering a conventional bachelor party. DON'T! The bachelor party is an event arranged by a young man's "best friends" with the sole intention of getting him laid and/or embarrassed by some STD-laden, pole-dancing ho that was scooped up to "loosen up" the guys. The guys. The groom's buddies. Translation: a potpourri of assholes who enjoy the imagined persona of being a big shot for one night. Cigars, shots, hoots and hollers. Don't do it.

Look at the antipodal themes of the shower versus the bachelor party. Think. What are the differences? Simple. Hello versus good-bye. Shower: hello wifehood. Bachelor party: good-bye happiness, freedom, excitement, maleness. Good-bye, old chap. And, oh yes, the nubile sylph sliding vaginally along a pole is the last one you'll ever have the vaguest chance at conquering. That is, without having your balls yanked from your scrotum with pliers.

Again, young male marriage first-timers, don't even think about it.

While we're talking about parties, where would a wedding be without a reception? Let's face it. The only thing getting your guests through the dreaded ceremony is the reception immediately thereafter. Let me stress that there should always be booze at a reception. Now, this may fascinate some, but in the South, Southern Baptists have been known to eschew hooch (forgetting, obviously, Jesus's first miracle). This is a mortal sin punishable by perpetual fire. Go ahead. Give your guests the rubber chicken. Humiliate the unmarried adults by making them sit at the singles' table.

Let everyone do the chicken dance. Just give them some alcohol to get through it all!

We're not finished, though.

Let's go back to the dementia of the wedding industry. Just walk through any magazine store and be amazed at the seemingly endless variety of bridal magazines. Magazines that have configured every possible permutation of theme. *N.B.* There are no groom magazines. Sorry, bucko, you don't even count. One of the true horrors of my life—next to a cystoscopy—was being dragged to a bridal fair. I'd rather go to a NAMBLA convention stag than attend one of these babies. A tribute to unmitigated inane largess. Various wedding purveyors display their wares. Get this. Ice carvers. Yep, ice carvers. And you thought buying a dress you only wear once was idiotic, try explaining shelling out a large for craftwork that MELTS! At least with the cake, you can freeze the top layer and, I dunno, attempt to eat it a year later, but this is evanescence at its most ludicrous.

Doves. I kid you not, you can rent doves to be released symbolizing God only knows what. DOVES!

And don't forget, when you send out invitations they must be addressed by a calligrapher. Better yet, why not have the calligraphically addressed invites delivered by a powdered-wig baron on his trusty steed. The psychosis called the wedding has no bounds. There's nothing too ludicrous.

How about gift registries? Nothing screams, "Oh, come

on!" more than having the unmitigated audacity to tell the hapless guests where they should waste their money in paying down a collection of whatever SHE picked out. Note that there's no liquor-store registry for the groom. Now, that would make sense. What better way to start a life together than with a well-stocked bar?

True story: A buddy of mine got hitched and his nut-job wife enclosed a registry card in the invite. I called up the department store and asked if anything on the list required many, many units. Say, for example, a lobster delivery system with one hundred tiny forks and Sterno holders. I ordered just three forks and the Sterno holder. Priceless.

Let's look at the procession down the aisle. Bridey is not walked or escorted, she's dragged. Remember, she's wearing white. The "virgin" is being sacrificed. Daddy Dearest then hands her off to the unsuspecting dolt who doesn't walk down any processional line, but just pops into the scene from offstage. Daddy-O tosses his theretofore dependent over to numb-nuts and the fun begins.

The two look at each other longingly. Actually, the groom's so hungover from the night before he's strabismic. Then the lies begin.

They promise, no, SWEAR, that they'll be together forever. Right. Just like the 54 percent of first-timers who uttered that tall tale before their marriage crashed in flames. They actually say those words, which we've all committed to memory much like Miranda warnings. What the groom should say is something like this:

I swear and affirm that I am absolutely aware of the fact that this is the last piece of ass I will ever have. That's it. No one else. And I hereby acknowledge that I am aware of the fact that I will never again gaze upon the naked form of a new and different chick that I've whiskied into a one-nighter. I understand that I will never again know that warm feeling that comes over me when I realize that I'm about to get laid . . . by someone new. I hereby swear and affirm that I will ditch all secreted porn including the Christy Canyon retrospective tribute box set. I further acknowledge that the form my bride-to-be is currently exhibiting on this special and artificially rare day could and most probably will change drastically, her physiognomy forever changing into the couch-like shape exhibited by her beast of a mother sitting in the front row glaring at me. Furthermore, I acknowledge that when this American dream of marriage transmutes into parenthood, there is a virtual certainty that the pert lass next to me will morph into a mom, her body forever changed, the victim of gravity, lactation, and myriad hormonal and post-partum stresses that I shan't and can't possibly ever understand. I hereby acknowledge and attest that I willfully and knowingly accept her parents as my new non-consanguineous appendage via affinity.

I'm not being cynical, but realistic. You see, as anyone with a gram of sentience is aware, men aren't raised or (better) "groomed" to look dreamy-eyed at the notion of being married. It just doesn't happen. The inculcation that women experience via this societal and peer reinforcement is not known in the male world. That's why most men who marry, especially at an early age, do so out of a fear that their women will move on for that ever-illusive "commitment." Oh, yeah, the commitment. That's chick-speak for the wedding. Again, not the marriage, the wedding.

So ingrained in American women is the necessity of marriage that it has become a cultural theme. In the film *When Harry Met Sally* there's a scene where the gals are chatting and one admits that she's getting divorced. The most prophetic line ever enunciated on screen is the retort from one of the friends who quips, "Yeah, but at least you can say you were married." I remember a female friend of mine years ago considering blowing off a high school reunion because she never married. Needless to say, she ultimately went and was the belle of the ball as her singleness magnetically attracted virtually all of the men in attendance. She viewed herself as single; the men saw her as unscathed.

You can't get a driver's license in this country without being tested for moderate proficiency in traffic laws. But to get married, you needn't exhibit even a *de minimis* appreciation for the laws that accompany this union. Now, I'm not suggesting marriage permits or certificates of marital-jurisprudence proficiency, but you'd think people would have a better idea of what this very important event legally entails. Nah! That would just make sense.

Ladies, it ain't just the wedding. That's merely the precursor. The personality changes that occur between the ages of twenty and thirty are unfathomable. This knight in shining armor will one day end up asleep on the couch in a beer buzz, his erstwhile six-pack now reduced to a party ball. He'll fart in keys the human ear can't decipher. This once-sex-crazed lothario will become all but abstemious. Familiarity breeds contempt. You'll find each other becoming brother and sister and then father and daughter, mother and son. Women will find a maternal instinct that lay dormant and now consumes them.

Hubby will feel a degree of resentment. This is when both of you may consider looking elsewhere to rekindle the feelings that brought you together in the first place. Women will crave romance again and may consider sex as a conduit for love. Men very well may use the hallucination of love to get sex. He'll want to feel virile again, that he still has it. Women will feel the ravages of age—always being foist upon her by the cosmetics industry and *Entertainment Tonight*—and may be sideswiped emotionally by the younger man who notices sexuality in her that has been suppressed, ignored, and overlooked. Men, you might want to pay a surprise visit to your wife's gym. Take a look at that personal "trainer."

Men, pick up any ladies' magazine. Read in amazement the number of articles that promise ten quick ways to spice up a marriage. Women really are concerned.

Remember the classic joke: Why do women fake orgasms? Because they think we care.

So here's the drill. Women, enjoy your wedding but remember that is just the proem to a life—a LIFE—together.

Men, get your heads out of your arses and pay attention.

God, it's so great being an expert.

A CLOSE SHAVE

My father had a beard like barbed wire. Let me describe. Nails through skin. Not Abe Lincoln. Not Edmund Gwenn in *Miracle on 34th Street*. Not even Grizzly Adams. But whiskers upon which you could strike a match or sand wood. Got it? I mean, he'd grow a beard in an hour. Five o'clock shadow? No. Shadow. Period.

I marveled at the procedure he went through each morning. A Gillette razor and a Wilkinson blade. Nothing safety about it. Cut yourself and you bled to death. A manly shave. Straight razors and barbers may have gone the way of pleurisy, but this was still plenty dangerous. This was the new and improved implement for taking your life into your hands. A palmful of Barbasol and a prayer. Dear God, let me not hit a vital blood structure. You had to push in at first to make contact. You always did this away from scar-obvious portions of the maw. It cracked, it scraped. How anyone ever made it through a morn's shave was and is still an amazement to me. Styptic pencils (whatever they were) for the brave at heart and wadded up toilet paper both stanched the blood. This looked like fun, I so stupidly thought. My father looked at me and said in a sinister "you'll see" tone, "You're gonna hate this."

No truer words were ever said. Some ask, why do I sport a beard? After my father was done sopping up the clotted blood shards and convincing the EMS techs my mother had called that immediate hospital transport was not required, he'd take that blade, that microtome, and delicately deposit it into that slit in the back of the medicine cabinet. What's that thing called? That receptacle, that repository of blood-caked blades? If you're old enough to know you *are* old.

And he was right. So right. I hate shaving, so I don't.

WHO ORDERED THE VEAL CUTLET?

There are two punch lines that I love. I don't know who first said them, so I haven't a clue as to whom I should credit.

Whenever I hear someone say something that is inarticulate, unintelligible, or just plain stupid, and I want to provide a retort that confuses them, establishes my disinterest, and cracks me up all at the same time, I respond with, "Wear a long coat and nobody will notice."

Any statement.

Any comment.

Anything. I just respond with this great instruction and walk off. It accomplishes nothing other than to confuse the hell out of everyone. And I love confusion.

This line connotes a need to deceive and conceal. To obfuscate and camouflage. It's covert and it's also a little bit sexual—inappropriately sexual. A mentulate flasher requiring a Chesterfield coat to hide Mother Nature. Nah, that's not for me. But it's still a great line.

Now, as to the veal.

When I'm trying to suggest that someone is in a stupor or confused or addled by dementia or just plain crazy, I will ofttimes say that so-and-so all the while was hollering "Who ordered the veal cutlet?" Translation: They're daft, out of it, loaded, crazy, misinformed. A radio program director. It signals that someone is out of their mind.

And we are.

All of us.

Out of our minds.

MAYBERRY, USA

Being from Florida, I've seen some real beauts when it comes to legislation proscribing the innocent and the inane, especially in my hometown, Tampa. They must have a lot of time on their hands in Tampa; what else could explain these low moments of legislative renaissance?

There's what I lovingly refer to as the Oscar Meyer Mandate. Apparently local lawmakers once found it offensive for thong bikini–clad hot dog vendors to ply their wiener wares by the side of the road, actually a causeway where other thong bikini–clad women sunbathed. What was the distinction? There was none. Daft legislators inferred a nexus between wiener vending and traffic problems. I don't get it either. It seems that these prudes just couldn't stand these thronged vendors (insert your own bun pun) vending so they came up with some convoluted scenario whereby the vendors would distract motorists and roadway carnage would ensue. I don't know. Beats the fuck out of me still. But they tried everything because these chicks were sexy or something.

Here's another example. One anorgasmic postmenopausal legislatrix heard of a bar whose waitresses wore bikinis. Bikinis. Not nude. Bikinis. The harridan thought this would excite and rile the sexual flames of the bars' soused patrons to such an extent that they might accost young girls who attended an adjacent dance school. I kid you not. She tried and tried to close this bar down. Why, you ask? Because, again, sexy women are bad.

I recall another city statute that prohibited women from loitering and/or prowling for the purposes of "inducing" fellatio, cunnilingus, or sodomy. (I don't recall intercourse being mentioned.) This is more indirect. This statute suggests that these unnatural acts weren't being offered; no, that would make sense. No, the loitering and prowling would somehow *induce* said acts to be committed. What prompted this statutory monstrosity? Seems that a contingent of hookers had moved into a neighborhood and were seen waving at motorists to alert them of their available services. The trollops were adorned in their usual strumpet garb and this annoyed their neighbors. So, the city made it a crime to wave. Repeat, to wave. Because, the legislators thought, they knew it wasn't a usual harmless wave, but a howdy-do that would inspire sodomy.

One statute forbade anyone from being or *appearing* nude in public. That's right, appearing. Say you were wearing flesh-colored tights in public (think shady Renaissance festival) and it looked or appeared as though you were nude. You were guilty of violating the statute.

But the biggest and most ridiculous piece of legislation to come out of Tampa involves one of my heroes, Joe Redner.

Joe is the owner and purveyor of the Mons Venus in Tampa, Florida. Mons Venus is the Mecca of lap dancing. A venue where nubile sylphs hang from poles and beg for dollars. A place where horny guys go and pay lots of money to stare at women who dance and prance about nekkid. It is believed that Joe invented the lap dance. OK, I'll pretend that you've never heard of a lap dance and define it. A lap dance involves a nude gal gyrating and grinding near or on your lap while you sit in a darkened corner of the bar. You can't touch her in any way, but her nether regions may come into contact with your lap. This takes place until . . . well, its conclusion, which can be negotiated either via elapsed time or certain events that, er, *come* to fruition. The lap dancer then tucks a Jackson or a Grant twixt her whatever(s) and that's that.

Sounds dreadful, doesn't it? Well, it certainly did to some

of Tampa's city fathers, who for years tried to legislate away the specter of the lap dance. God knows the money wasted by the government to arrest Redner, his patrons, and the girls themselves. They even went so far as to devise a rule whereby patrons could not approach within six feet of an unclothed hottie. This kinda ruins the propinquity element of the lap dance, but that was the idea. Hours were wasted debating the proximity of dancer and patron. Vice cops were secreted in the club to keep a watchful eye on patrons. What a job! They'd sit for hours nursing a drink that they never sipped (Clue #1) and spy on guys getting danced on. Danced *over*? *At?* Whatever. I guess that residential burglary and child abduction were under control. This lap dancing detail was mucho important.

The City of Tampa was safe; the lap dance was curtailed. Politicians went further citing imaginary statistics linking prostitution with such establishments. Time, money, all was wasted because of this. And no one uttered a peep. No politician had the wherewithal (translation: balls) to say this was insane. But Joe fought and now counts his millions, thanks to the closed-minded insanity of a few do-gooders. God knows what Joe paid in lawyers and bail bondsmen or how many times he and his girls were arrested. This guy's the Rosa Parks of nude dancing and artistic expression. Yeah, artistic expression. Look it up!

Most of these idiot Tampa pols have left or been voted out of office. Nude dancing continues, bigger than ever. The Mons, like the Alamo, still stands. And Joe has entered the pantheon of great men fighting for our right to, uh, you know.

I'M A *YEAHBUT*

On my first day of law school, one of my professors told the class it would be a sure thing that we'd be at a party and someone would hear that we were in law school. (He said "would hear" but really what he meant was "you are young and boastful and full of yourselves so you're going to make sure that everyone within earshot knows that you are in law school, you little asswipes." Lucky for us he left that part out.) The prof went on to say that chances were that that someone, the party of the first part, would then ask a question about something judicial which we, the party(ies) of the second part, would be obliged to answer.

Can I sue my landlord for a leaky faucet? Can George Bush be indicted for war crimes? Can I get off jury duty by saying that we should hang all criminals no matter what they're charged with? Can I sue Joan Rivers's plastic surgeon for malpractice?

What to say? What to answer? What to do without our law books and case studies and vending machines? The correct response, the prof advised, would answer every legal question perfectly. It would square all the issues. It would cover every angle. It would be concise and precise. Exquisite. Eloquent.

The answer, he intoned, was "It depends."

Smart man, our professor.

Few issues are simple. Nothing is apodictic, black or white. Nothing is even gray. Hell, there are shades of gray. Doesn't matter what the question is, the answer—all answers—are contingent on circumstances, invariables, variables, the zeitgeist, and the prevailing notions and doctrines. There is nothing that faces us today that is susceptible to a Manichean analysis. (And no, that doesn't come with noodles and an eggroll.)

Take an issue, say, abortion. Are you for abortion? *For?* No. Who's *for* abortion? What does that mean? Either the question is imprecise or the answer is irrelevant and inapposite. OK, than you're *against* abortion. No, wait! The process, the medical procedure? Keep parsing. OK, so are you asking me if I'm for the right to choose abortion? Yeah, OK. I'm for the right to choose abortion. So kids can abort a child? Wait! A *child*? Is the fetus a child? Wait! Is the fetus a human? What's a fetus? Wait! The child who's about to abort the fetus, er, child. How old is that child? You mean the kid who's pregnant? Yeah, that kid. Twelve. Twelve?! Wait! What was the original question?

You've heard that one before? OK, what about capital punishment? Do you value every human life? Yeah. What about Charles Manson? OK, all life but his. Should he receive the death penalty? Absolutely. But he didn't kill anyone. Yeah, but he *told* others to kill people. He *told* them?! Shouldn't they be indicted for being gullible as well as the murders *they* committed? Well, of course. Yeah, but you wanted to execute Charles Manson. OK, I changed my mind. When should anyone receive the death penalty? Well, it depends.

That's the way it goes for any issue. It will evolve and devolve and transmute and mutate and vary. There is nary an issue worth discussion that isn't complicated. Period.

So as to abortion, *yeah*, I believe a woman should have an unfettered right to reproductive freedom *but* there are conditions that must be placed on this right. But I'm ambivalent when it comes to a minor's right to have an abortion weighed against her parents' consent. A kid can't even be treated for lice without Mom and Dad's OK, but no such approval is needed for an abortion? It depends. What if the kid fears for her life if crazy Dad finds out she's pregnant?

Capital punishment? Yeah, I can see how the horrible

crimes committed by someone can inspire such anger and a desire for revenge, but in many cases we're convicting the wrong people. What to do? As far as people who yap it up on cell phones in movie theatres, I may make an exception. OK, maybe not the death penalty, but waterboarding may be in order.

This drives people batty. Talk radio and political commentary love absolutes. The airwaves are filled with absolutists, nonwavering folks who grab a label and try to affix it to everything. But that's nonsense. There isn't an issue that can be satisfied by the application of a label. There isn't an issue that doesn't deserve to be analyzed and evaluated.

As to these labels?

Am I a conservative? Nah. Silly. Conserving what? That's a synonym for stodgy, antediluvian, hoary, unimaginative.

Liberal? Equally stupid. That's become a code word for Democrat, a synomyn for some granola-eating, Birkenstock-wearing pussy.

I'm a registered Independent, an equally inane *party*. (Who's doing the catering? That's what I'd like to know.)

Progressive? Don't get me started. As opposed to retrogressive? Nonsense. Besides, it's an insurance company.

I then thought that "relativist" may make sense. Relative to the situation, the issue, the facts, the times, the whatever. Yeah, I liked it. "Relativist." Nope. No good. Too arcane, recondite. It seems so wishy-washy. So unsure. It also sounds too much like "moral relativism," the ideology of the godless and dreaded atheist.

So what am I?

I'm a *yeahbut.*

L-L-L-LIONEL AND THE JETS

I'm a stutterer.

I don't tell a lot of folks this because they don't have much interest, but stuttering is my handicap and I'm stuck with it. Mostly I've learned how to work around it—have even worked my way out of it—but I still feel it coming on at times and I've got to watch what words I use and how I use them.

Like most stutterers I have a hard time, a real hard time, saying certain words—target or trigger words, those that pose a particular problem in pronunciation. Words, for instance, that start with *l* are very tricky for me. So guess what my name is? Michael Lebron. First name ends in *l*, last name starts in *l*. That was a handicap. My name. Once, in the beginning of fifth grade, I think, a nun asked each of us to stand and say our names. I was watching in horror as each kid stood and announced his name. I felt dread as the announcers snaked towards me. I had to do something, so I stood and said, à la James Bond, "Lebron. Mike Lebron." I may have even spelled it. That seemed to work.

(Come to think of it, we were kids who'd been together since first grade. Why the need for an introduction now?)

I came up with a way of saying my name which I still use to this day. In my mind I said "uh" between my first and last name. Only I could hear it. Or think it. I was Michael "uh" Lebron. Subsonic. Imperceptible. That's me. I figured a way around the problem. Occasionally the "uh" was audible so "Lebron" sounded like "O'Brien." Sometimes I didn't correct people and to this day, it's an alias.

Hardly the springboard for loquacity, professional, no less. I once had a nun suggest to me that I was mentally retarded because of my "inability." Retarded?! It was the best thing that ever happened to me. I wanted to prove that old bat wrong, and I think I did. Trial lawyer, stand-up comic (Did I mention that?), talk-show host. And now. (Drum roll, maestro.) Author. Well, that's not fair; it's hard to stutter when you type. But give me a minute, I'll figure a way.

I was a fat kid too.

No, excuse me, big-boned, as my loving mother referred to me. I was also bespectacled and had braces (on my teeth) at the age of ten. A fat, braced stutterer with glasses.

I was a serial-killer-to-be.

Nice.

By the way, if you ever encounter a stutterer, never complete his sentence for him. It's usually a "him," for nature tends to make men more predisposed to this. (A woman with a stutter would be like a giraffe with a sore throat. Think about it. Nothing dare impede a woman's speaking ability. But I digress.) When encountering a stutterer, just wait. The poor guy knows he stutters without you finishing sentences for him. Well, in my book that's grounds for justifiable homicide.

Stutterers have come up with a variety of explanations for the disorder. My favorite was the one that suggested that my brain works so fast, my mouth can't keep up with my thoughts.

Goes to show you how creative stutterers are.

What about this one: a hemispheric battle in the brain. Left brain versus right. Speech versus imagery. That's a good one too. It's really fascinating. Stutterers can usually sing (think Mel Tillis) and can speak fine if they do it rhythmically. I found early on that if I spoke in an accent I'd get by. My parents would never even say they noticed how Chubby the Stutterer all of a sudden was sporting a Brooklynesque delivery.

What I think was the most important aspect of these circumstances—about who I was and who I am—is that I have this innate, almost atavistic, sentience and feeling for the underdog. The mistreated, the misunderstood. I've always seen the alternative, the different. I've always felt different. But in a good way. I developed early on a philosophy of, pardon me, "fuck 'em." Who cares what people thought? And it toughened me up yet never destroyed me.

Attta boy, Nietzsche.

NO CONCEPT

I was a prosecutor for the 13th Judicial Circuit in Hillsborough County, Florida (that would be Tampa). I represented the State of Flawda and saw and heard a lot that I've found to be rather funny. Hours of sitting in courtrooms hearing the pleas and averments of the flotsam and jetsam of society (and those are the judges, mind you) have given me a few memorable moments.

People think they are familiar with courtrooms. For this we can thank *Law and Order*. But trust me, they're not like that. Courtrooms are not "As Seen on TV," they are dreary, spooky, medieval, and cathedralesque places with a man wearing a robe (well, it's usually a man), a bailiff (translation: a bus driver with a gun) or two, a clerk, a probation officer, a court reporter, and scores of people scared shitless when they have to approach "the bench." Now I ask you: Where did this "bench" shit come from? When I hear bench, I think workbench, as in Santa and his elves. When a player is benched, he sits it out. Johnny Bench. OK, that was stupid. Dame Judy Bench. Now that was extremely stupid.

But let's focus.

On one occasion a defendant approached the *bench* and was asked a number of prefatory questions. As everyone with a patellar reflex knows, you call the judge "Your Honor." This one poor guy included within each statement to the bench "My Honor": "Thank you, My Honor." "Three bags full, My Honor." *My* Honor?! Let me say something about suppressed laughter. It's, well, suppressed, and anything that vaguely resembles funny in a court of law is exponentially elevated to hysterical. And this inspired hysterics.

I'm killing you, right? Well, you haven't heard this beaut.

Let's take pleas that are entered at an arraignment. Or, as one client called it, an *arrangement.* This was the hoot of the year when we comedically suppressed lawyers heard this classic. And it was so apropos. *Arrangement.*

Well, back to the show.

An arraignment takes place when a defendant in a criminal case is formally told of her charge. This is a needless vestige of common-law days when a defendant didn't know her charge. This is complete horseshit now. You see, after your arrest and being cuffed, you kind of have an inkling as to why you've been pinched and what the charge is. "You're under arrest for ____." And there you have it.

When you are brought before My Honor you can only plead *guilty, not guilty,* or *no contest.* That's it. The first two are self-explanatory. This third can cause a problem.

The no-contest plea (*nolo contendere*), in essence, is neither an admission nor a denial of a charge. It's your decision not to contest the matter *and* not admit it. I didn't say I did it; I didn't say I didn't. *Huh?* I'm just wishing not to contest or argue this matter. Let's just be done with it as though I pled guilty without my having admitted shit. Double *huh?* (Don't you wish you went to law school?)

The no-contest plea has no counterpart in the real world, by the way. We never plead *nolo* when arguing with bosses or spouses. A woman would never say, for example, "I'm not denying that I slept with the milkman. And I'm not admitting I slept with the milkman. And I'm not saying anything about the twelve pounds of cheese and the six gallons of milk in the fridge. I'm just *not contesting it.*"

It's critical to understand the no-contest plea. If, for example, you pay a traffic ticket where an accident was involved, you need to realize that by paying the traffic ticket you've just admitted guilt and are "not contesting" the matter. A no-contest plea however, would allow you to dispose of the matter but not admit to the underlying charge, e.g., speeding or careless driving. I can just see your eyes rolling back. Read on.

This is getting boring.

Now one more rule of criminal procedure before we get to comedy paydirt. Oh, it's coming; trust me. A judge must accept a plea to a charge only when there is no ambiguity as to what the defendant says and means as to the plea. This means that he must plead to a charge absolutely and perfectly clearly. "I plead guilty." "Not guilty, Your Honor." Those are specific. "Well, let me explain" is not a plea; it's ambiguous. It's called "I don't know what he's saying." It's guilty, not guilty, or no contest. Period.

Anything short of absolute clarity results in the judge entering a plea of "not guilty" and that means "set it for trial." And that's the last thing a trial judge with a huge docket or the poor guy being charged wants. Enough with trials! They clog the docket, especially when some poor schmoe just wants to dispose of his case.

A judge knows when some *idjit* wants to plead no contest but didn't rehearse it quite enough. (Remember, anything short of absolute clarity is entered as a not-guilty plea and that means trial and nobody wants that. OK, get ready to cachinnate.) Consider this: Once a defendant was trying to enter a plea of no contest. He almost had the phrase right, but not quite. The poor judge was trying to "help" the defendant in getting the name of the plea right, but he was limited from helping too much. The judge can assist but not prompt. Whatever the hell that means.

What transpired, I'll never forget. Here's the succession of no-contest plea attempts by this poor bastard. They're thematically referenced and catalogued:

"I plead *no context.*" This would be the contextual defense.

Oops, let's try it again.

"I plead *no comment.*" This would be the ostensible Fifth Amendment defense. You're getting closer . . . once more.

"I plead *no conscience.*" At last, the insanity defense.

That would be strike three.

Needless to say, the judge entered the plea as not guilty as was his duty. My Honor was pissed off by yet another case needlessly set for trial. The defendant was equally pissed because he wanted just to enter his *nolo*-whatever plea, pay the fine, and get the hell out of there.

And I laughed, documenting the event in a notebook to be referenced later for the book I would eventually write.

TOWARD A NEW THEORY
OF EVOLUTION

Men are classic scholars in evolution, makeshift mind you. Men can come up with a theory that philandering is normal, that monogamy is unnatural, that as hunters and gatherers we had to disseminate (literally) while the woman stayed home with the breed. That may be true for a timber wolf but it has no relevance today. Men, a little word of advice: Never, NEVER ever let a woman hear such insane blather. Look, Margaret Mead wannabes, shut up. Zip it. This is utter nonsense. True, there may be (again) some primordial or atavistic urge to conquer as many women as we can, but just as we've also conquered the instinct to steal food, this is conquerable as well.

BIGFOOT

You know what they say about girls with big feet . . .

Neither do I. Let's move on.

Bigfoot is the greatest example of man's penchant to wax mystical. He provides an analogue as to how we continue to believe, *believe*, in the utterly preposterous and impossible.

Bigfoot or Sasquatch and its offshoot Yeti (second cousins twice removed, I think) are amalgams of a hairy, bipedal hominid that somehow slipped through the cracks of evolution and extinction. A resilient character too tough to die off. The missing link. The classically themed ape. King Kong. Mighty Joe Young. And don't forget the reverse theme: Tarzan, the human who refuses to evolve, thus maintaining his/our primordial, atavistic self. It's fascinating.

I recall reading of a true American hero, Ray Wallace,

who, according to his kids, swore them to secrecy until his death in 2002. This may also be mythical, but I love the idea even if it's bullshit. Seems that ol' Ray was a prankster and carved wooden feet that he would use to leave footprints, giant imprints, around northern California. God, I hope this is true. There were additional stories suggesting that family members may have donned an ape suit and walked around to be filmed via that now universally accepted cinema technique, the grainy home video. When I see images of the alleged Bigfoot walking around, it's still interesting to note how this perhaps pseudo-simian walks remarkably upright, his gait almost nonchalant, traipsing with an ostensible "pissed-off" countenance. Let me reiterate, I am not a journalist, have not verified anything contained herein, and admonish you to imagine that the term "alleged" precedes every sentence and noun. That being said, it does make sense. After all, a seven-foot hominid gallivanting around completely undetected for how many years?

Since the fifties?

Yet believers press on.

Our imaginations are fecund. That's what separates us from our porcine friends—other than a corkscrewed dick. But I can only speak for myself.

The very idea of Bigfoot is evidence of a collective affirmation that we as humans enjoy. And it just goes to show that the most outlandish claims gain legitimacy when practiced and endorsed by a large group of people. Sure, Sasquatch may seem silly in the here and now, alone with your thoughts and a six-pack. But simply go to a Sasquatch convention and all of a sudden it seems less crazy. How can I be nuts if so many others believe in what is arguably far-fetched? All these people can't be wrong. Just look at religion. Snake-handling may seem a tad out there unless and until you celebrate such with a congregation of serpent devotees.

Makes you think, doesn't it?